Praise for
Unwanted No More

BJ's unpacking of her life reminds us all of our brokenness. You'll discover in her journey how fullness of life can come to any of us, no matter our situations. Don't miss the gift revealed on the pages of this book.

—Jeff Pinkerton
Author, *Common Sense to Uncommon Wealth*

Rarely is someone emotionally equipped to share so transparently the wounding coming from a broken childhood in a broken world. BJ not only captures those stories in a riveting way but draws the eager reader forward to discover how God walks believers through healing and into a life that glorifies Him. You won't want to stop once you begin!

—Linda Lesniewski
Author, *Women at the Cross* and *Connecting Women*

B. J. Garret's memoir is sure to tug your heart. An honest and forthright account of hard beginnings turned glorious through Christ's redemptive work. Readers will be encouraged as well as challenged to examine their own lives to see how God brings us to places we could never hope or imagine. Kudos, BJ and Redemption Press.

—Linda Wood Rondeau
Author, speaker

B. J. Garrett is a very real trophy of God's amazing grace. Through God's power, she has grown into a brilliant diamond that reflects the light of her beloved Savior, Jesus. My friend, my sister in Christ, BJ's journey will be an inspiration to everyone.

—Sam DeVille
Senior pastor, Flint Baptist Church

Unwanted No More by B. J. Garrett is a Romans 8:28 story if I've ever read one. From the first page to the last, every heartbreak and loss, every bit of abuse and shame, and every lie whispered to her young heart and leaving her feeling unwanted, God used for good in the end. Recounted with such transparency, her excruciating childhood of being sinned against time and time again prepared her to sin against others. But God was pursuing her all along the way. The transformation of BJ's heart of stone into a tender and compassionate heart toward God and the lost is a sight to behold. I just could not get enough of this story. It drew me in and would not let me go. What a testimony to a Savior who can truly make all things new!

—Athena Dean Holtz,
Publisher, author, speaker, former radio host

Genuine self-disclosure is a powerful tool for counseling ministry. B. J. Garrett discloses her story to help others facing a life filled with loneliness and guilt due to abandonment, abuse, or the emotional aftermath of abortion. Well-written and compelling, *Unwanted No More* also proclaims her experience of God's acceptance, love, and leadership.

—Ronnie J. Johnson, PhD
Professor of Christian education and counseling,
Baptist Missionary Association Theological Seminary

I love how BJ drew me in to her story. It is a beautiful picture of God's redemptive power and grace that reaches even the darkest valley to rescue the perishing. *Unwanted No More* lifts our eyes to the Savior—the Lord Jesus Christ. He is the Way, the Truth, and the Life (John 14:6).

—Tina Craighead
Still Waters Ministry, Tennessee

It wasn't pretty—far from it. From mess to Messiah, *Unwanted No More* is a story of REDEMPTION told with the transparency of Saran Wrap. The rejection, abuse, cruelty, and condemnation BJ suffered at the hands of those who were supposed to protect her is heartbreaking. From tear soaked to fear cloaked to faith filled, this book is PROOF that the impossible is possible with God. I could not put it down!

—Tammy Whitehurst
Professional speaker and co-owner of the
Christian Communicators Conference

BJ's snippets of memories and scenes of her past take the reader into her deepest, darkest secrets of rejection, violence, and abuse. Once promiscuity, cheating, and failure . . . now clean, really clean. From my body and my choice to living fully present in every season. A frothy pineapple punch of a story depicting God's providence of love multiplied.

—Blanton Feaster, PhD
Vice president of Executive Affairs

UNWANTED
No More

From Exploited to Embraced by God

Ann,

Oh how I adore you!

Love,

RJ Jarrett

UNWANTED
No More

From Exploited to Embraced by God

B. J. Garrett

Foreword by Christine Hoover

Published by Redemption Press, PO Box 427, Enumclaw 98022.

Toll-Free (844) 2REDEEM (273-3336)

Redemption Press is honored to present this title in partnership with the author. The views expressed or implied in this work are those of the author. Redemption Press provides our imprint seal representing design excellence, creative content, and high-quality production.

All Scripture quotations, unless otherwise indicated, are taken from the *Holy Bible, New International Version*®. *NIV*®. Copyright © 1973, 1978, 1984 by International Bible Society. Used by permission of Zondervan. All rights reserved.

The author has tried to recreate events, locales, and conversations from her memories of them. In order to maintain their anonymity, in some instances she has changed the names of individuals and may have changed some identifying characteristics and details, such as physical properties, occupations, and places of residence.

Image by Clker-Free-Vector-Images from Pixabay

ISBN 13: 978-1-68314-944-6 (Paperback)
978-1-68314-945-3 (ePub)
978-1-68314-946-0 (Mobi)

Dedication

For my sister, Mandy.
Your love, protection, and support
have molded me into who I am.

Contents

Foreword

Every Christian has a story to tell. Although our names and experiences are plastered throughout, our stories are ultimately not about us but rather are about the power of God to save sinners through the life, death, and resurrection of Jesus.

This book is BJ's story, a riveting and often harrowing account of poverty, abuse, repercussions of sin, and a desperate search for belonging. BJ holds nothing back, revealing the dark world she lived in for so long and the darkest choices she made. She tells it all because, as will quickly become clear, she's experienced true release from shame and guilt through the grace of God. This is His story displayed through her life.

I first heard BJ's story when she was a guest on my podcast, By Faith. I listened, amazed, as she recounted her life experiences. I knew as we talked that day that so many women listening would be able to relate to the parts of her story that include abortion and sexual abuse, and I knew they'd be challenged by her ability to both receive forgiveness from God and give forgiveness to her abusers.

When BJ told me afterward that she'd known for some time that she needed to obey God by writing her story for a wider audience—something she'd started but never finished—I encouraged her to continue on. And I'm so glad she did!

You will be glad as well as you read these pages. You may not have a story like BJ's. My story, though filled to the brim with rules and religion, mirrors the same pride and self-oriented living characterized by the licentiousness in BJ's life. My life might have looked better on the outside, but in God's eyes, my religious actions were only rubbish. In Philippians 3 Paul says that in our life apart from Christ, whether religious or rebellious, nothing gains us favor with God. The only résumé, so to speak, that gains us anything with God is Christ's alone. All before in our lives is loss; the gain of righteousness and God's love is found in Christ. BJ has discovered this beautiful truth, and my prayer as you read her story is that you'll discover it too.

Christine Hoover
Author, podcaster, Bible teacher

Introduction

"I know the plans I have for you," declares the Lord,
"plans to prosper you and not to harm you,
plans to give you hope and a future."
Jeremiah 29:11

We all love a good story. That's likely why you picked up this book in the first place. A well-told story can take you back in time, bring you to hysterical laughter, or overwhelm your heart with such intense emotion it's as if you were part of the experience. In these pages, you'll find relatable emotions, desires, fears, accomplishments, and dreams.

Why am I writing this book? I've been asked that question many times by those I've shared my secret desires with and by those from whom I sought help with the task. I've asked myself the question too, as I've spent hours in self-doubt, wallowing in a sea of emotional sludge. I do not consider myself a writer. I'm a terrible speller with terrible grammar. I am uneducated by the world's standards. Why me? Why my story? With all the amazing stories available, truth or fiction, why must I write mine?

The answer is, because the Lord told me to.

So in obedience, I began. Today, as I opened this manuscript for the bazillionth time—questioning, feeling uncertain, insecure, and simply wondering why the Lord commissioned me to write this—I began by reading Jeremiah 29:11. It reminded me to trust that this book is His plan and that despite my own fears, no plan of His will harm me; it will only be for my good. And God's Word strengthened my faith that in my obedience, this divine call on my heart would be accomplished.

As you read my heart poured out on the page, you will know my deepest, darkest secrets. Things I did. Things that were done to me. Things that crippled me emotionally and spiritually for most of my life. Maybe you will relate to some of my story. I hope that in reading my story, you will realize that you also have a story to tell.

Whatever you've done, whatever has been done to you—you matter. Your life matters because you have a purpose and because you were created by a holy, loving creator God who adores you. A God who wants a real relationship with you. A God who, quite literally, died so you could live an abundant life for all eternity. Unless you see Jesus interwoven throughout, I have failed.

If the Lord will use a story like mine, I promise you, He can use a story like yours. We are in this together, and like me, Jesus has big plans for you!

You created my inmost being; you knit me together in my mother's womb. I praise you because I am fearfully and wonderfully made; your works are wonderful, I know that full well. My frame was not hidden from you when I was made in the secret place, when I was woven together in the depths of the earth. Your eyes saw my unformed body; all the days ordained for me were written in your book before one of them came to be.

Psalm 139:13–16

Chapter 1

Stormy Beginnings

My grandson, Aiden, squirmed against the cushion of the mahogany booth and reached for another warm, flaky cheddar biscuit, sending crumbs across his coloring sheet. Our visit to Red Lobster's all-you-can-eat shrimp extravaganza had become a birthday tradition. The familiar shiplap walls and smell of seafood always took me back to the memorable day when a baby boy came home with a hurricane.

"Aiden, do you remember why the day you were born was so special?"

He responded with a mouth still full of biscuit. "Because of the big storm."

I paused as a waiter refilled our drinks.

"That's right. You had to stay at the hospital a few extra days because of Hurricane Ike."

Not that the delay had mattered as I sat on that teal hospital couch, holding the sweetest bundle of perfection I had ever seen. Sure, massive sheets of rain pounded the window behind me, power was out all over town, and trees were being snapped in half or uprooted—it didn't matter. My heart was overflowing with an intense love for this brown-eyed baby boy holding my pinky finger in his wrinkled little hands.

He was here. We were safe. Named for my husband, Aiden Jay Green had already captured my heart. The raging love of this nana for her first grandchild bested the storm.

The waiter stopped by again, this time to slide a steaming platter of shrimp onto our table.

"When we finally brought you home," I continued, "we had no electricity. We were all so hungry that we decided to go eat at Red Lobster while we waited for the power to come back on. So that's why we come every year—to remember."

My daughter, Ashlei, wiped a smear off Aiden's mouth with a napkin and ruffled his hair.

"Yes." Ashlei laughed, rolling her eyes in mock disgust. "What a day that was!"

Aiden scribbled a crayon across his sheet of paper, more interested in his drawing than in the details of his birth. But I held the details close, never wanting to forget the story that made his birthday as special and significant as he is.

The storm had begun long before the day he was born. Ashlei, seventeen and in love with her high school sweetheart, had moved out long enough to get her heart broken and to get pregnant. For days after she returned home, I sobbed under the bed covers, grieved about how having a child would alter her life. I knew all too well what you had to give up as a teen mother. I knew the cynical stares and judgmental looks she and her child would receive. I knew the mountains of baggage that came from stepping outside of God's design for sexuality. I knew the challenges of single parenting and the destruction it could cause to both their hearts.

I also worried about how this pregnancy would alter *my* life. What would people say? A church youth director with a teenage daughter pregnant out of wedlock? Why would the parents of my students want me to continue teaching their students when I had failed my own child so completely?

This was not the way I had pictured grandparenting. But that day, sitting in a Red Lobster after a storm with a tiny bundle of pure joy, my heart was beyond full. The love I had for him was bigger than any love I'd ever felt in my life. Different. Unlike me, he was wanted.

Ashlei had never considered abortion, and I had hope that my daughter would not have the same experience as I'd had. She had Jay and me and a church community as a support system. I could celebrate, knowing how much better life would be for Aiden than it had been for his mother and for me.

I relished the tradition of retelling my grandson's unique birth story because my own birth story had meant so much to me. For as long as I could remember, I'd been told about the spectacular moment in sports history on the day my mother brought me into the world: the longest ever doubleheader in baseball. Every year my aunt called or wrote to repeat the story.

"Out of all my nieces and nephews, your birth is the one that I remember the best. Grandma and I were at a Yankees game, and it turned out to be the longest doubleheader in the history of baseball. Grandma kept checking with the hospital to see how much time we had before we needed to get back. You waited to make your appearance until the game was over. As a die-hard Yankees fan, I appreciated that!"

Despite my ugly childhood, this story somehow made the day I was born seem monumental and meaningful. Little else in my life made me feel validated, so I pinned my significance on this special connection. Even as an adult, I clung to it. I wanted Aiden's story to make him feel special too.

That night, after a delicious, hurricane-free shrimp dinner, I decided to Google the date of my birth, just for fun. I wasn't expecting some flashing billboard to pop up with my birth announcement, but I did expect to find something about this astonishing sports feat.

Nothing.

I searched again. Maybe I needed to use different keywords.

Still nothing.

I frantically searched every way I knew how to look. It had to be on the web somewhere. I'd been told this story my entire life. But the details I did find didn't line up. The games in question had occurred the day before my birthday. And while it was a doubleheader, it wasn't the longest in history. Nothing about the games was remarkable or special.

The realization that this story wasn't true began to sink in. Each empty search brought suffocation to my lungs. The tears of despair finally made their way to my eyes as I sat battling within, trying desperately to hold them back. My world crashed over me in waves, and with it, my self-worth. I knew it was silly to feel so emotionally tied to a simple story, but it was the one consistent thing in my life, the one thing that had made me feel wanted—like my birth had meant something. The tiny shred of significance I had held had just drowned in a sea of false existence. The one story I had was a lie, and that made me feel like my entire life was a lie. The day I was born wasn't significant to anyone, not even a group of strangers watching baseball.

Worse, my aunt later denied ever having told me the story. Her rejection stung as much as anything. I pulled up her old messages, desperate to prove I hadn't made it up. The validation didn't wash away the heartbreak I still felt. Somewhere inside me, a little girl hadn't fully healed from the hurts of her childhood. Now, my birth story joined other missing memories in the void.

Memories of my childhood danced across my mind like footage from an old movie projector. Early images in black and white, scratchy, shaky, and blurred, gave way to a vivid, fast-moving film I could not slow down.

Whirr, clickety-clack . . .

I'm riding bareback as my father holds the reins of the pony's bridle. He's here. I cling to the feeling of being Daddy's little girl.

Whirr, click . . .

We're living in a tent at Lake Tawakoni. My sister protectively shields me as we walk to the shower. I am dirty.

Whirr, click . . .

I'm surrounded by drunkenness, cigarette smoke, and wild women. Police burst in, making arrests. Darkness whispers. Fear as thick as tar holds me captive.

Whirr, click . . .

I'm alone again. When will Mom be home? Unwanted. Why am I not wanted?

Whirr, click . . .

Snippets of memories and scenes of my past flashed through my heart and mind, but massive gaps in the film, like black holes, threatened to suck me in. I'd been struggling most of my life to piece my memories together and make sense of the ugliness that crowded my mind whenever they came up. Maybe those gaps were for my own self-preservation—a defense mechanism designed to protect me from pain. But what I couldn't remember frightened me, because the cold, paralyzing blankness of those black holes still evoked all the emotions of being abandoned and unloved, even when I couldn't bring a specific experience to mind. Somehow, the absent memories said as much as the ones remembered. In most of my memories, my mother was missing.

I had no snapshots of my mother cooking me breakfast—or any meal. I couldn't picture her in the kitchen or donning an apron. I saw only my hungry five-year-old self standing on a chair to reach the stove, cooking dinner for myself.

I had no memories of my mother fixing my hair—no braids or cute bows. I saw only the horrible haircuts and choppy bangs she gave me.

I had no memories of bedtime baths or of my mother tucking me in at night. I could see my older sister, Mandy, doing these things, but not my mother.

I had no memories of sweet, proud gestures of any kind. No playing dress-up, no walks in the park, no chaperoned school parties or field trips. When I was very young, my mother was simply not there. An abusive father and absent mother had twisted my experience of love, and I'd struggled with self-esteem my whole life. Now, this hurricane of the soul sucked me in, but unlike Aiden, I didn't know how the story ended.

21

Chapter 2

Hunting for Home

Muffled sirens wailing in the distance outside a faded light-pink motel. Chipping paint. Windows covered with rusted bars. A flickering, half-lit vacancy sign. I was about three years old, living alone with my father. A few days? A week? A month? I had no idea how long my father and I called this our home. All I knew was the one-bed motel room smelled stale and felt empty. My mother wasn't there, likely in jail again. My big sister, Mandy, wasn't there either—probably with other members of our family, since my father wasn't her father. I missed her. She took care of me. Protected me.

Once, my father took me to visit my mother in jail. There were muffled sirens in the distance there too. A small, stale, one-bed cell. Bars between us. It wasn't that different from our motel room. The security officers sat behind a desk, eating fried chicken. Mom had some too. My mouth watered. We'd only been there a few minutes when my mother and father began arguing. Their voices drowned out the music playing over the speaker system.

"You used your government assistance money to buy the fried chicken? That was supposed to be for Billy Jo!" Dad shook one of the bars with his fist.

"Billy Jo looks like she's doing fine with you. Why should I not enjoy nice food once in a while? I need to eat too." Mom smoothed her shapeless, billowy dress and took another bite of chicken.

Dad gestured toward her large frame and fired back. "Right, like you need fried chicken." There was no question that my mother was obese.

I stepped over to the cell and tugged on my father's pant leg. "Can I have some?" A whiff of terrible body odor overwhelmed the smell of fried chicken as I drew near. I wrinkled my nose. Mom didn't smell nice.

"C'mon, Billy Jo. We're going." Dad grabbed my hand and yanked me away.

As it turned out, Dad was leaving more than just the jail. He was leaving us. When my mother got out of jail, she took me and Mandy back. One day, Dad was there, and the next, he wasn't. I blamed my mother. Dad had openly hated her, so clearly it was her fault that he wasn't around. I was sure my father wanted me, but my mother? She didn't want me enough to stay out of jail. With my father no longer around, Mandy and I both were given away to family members each time my mother stole a purse, cigarettes, someone's identity—it didn't matter what. She wasn't very good at it, because she kept getting caught.

We lived with Uncle Dan for about six months and another time with Uncle Mark and Aunt Lynn. Our grandparents took us in off and on. We lived with cousin Judy and her husband for a full summer. Judy and Aunt Betty taught me to can tomatoes. For the first time in my life, that summer I felt safe, loved, and protected.

Then it was back to my mother. Back to roach-infested houses with no hot water—or no water at all—and sometimes, no electricity. Back to dirty clothes and lice in my eyebrows. Back to loud beater cars that smoked polluting fumes from the tailpipe and the hood. We were *that* family—the one that always needed help paying bills, always needed food, always need-ed a ride. We went to whatever church was currently helping us.

My mother pulled me through the door of the latest church office. "Can we speak to the pastor?" she asked sweetly.

I saw the familiar gleam of pity in the secretary's eyes as she looked at me.

"He'll be right with you."

The pastor wore a nice shirt and tie, even though it was the middle of the week. My clothes were especially tattered this morning. He led us to his office and gestured toward some chairs across from his desk.

"What can I do for you?"

My mother smoothed back my uneven bangs in an act of affection, tears in her eyes. "I want to ask about your benevolence fund. We're really struggling."

I slumped in the chair, propping my elbow on the arm and resting my chin in my hand. I'd seen this act before. My mother was a charmer, the kind of person who could woo someone into nearly anything. She was likable; everyone adored her until she stole from them or manipulated them to get what she wanted. I was the bait—a poor, scruffy daughter put on display simply to draw sympathy.

It worked, because churches often paid our bills or gave us food. I learned that church was the place to go when I was in trouble or needed help. But after watching my mother manipulate the generosity of others, I also learned that I'd rather cut off my big toe than ask for help. I didn't want to be anything like her.

We attended church regularly on Sunday mornings and Wednesday nights, but we never stayed at one place long enough to build any real relationships. I got baptized at every church we attended. In my mind, baptism was what you had to do to become a member of a church. I didn't understand what it really meant. I liked church, mostly because people were nice to me. I craved nice. Though I wanted to hide in the shadows and remain unnoticed, in my heart I craved attention and longed for someone to love me. At church I felt the love and provision I missed at home. I wanted what the church people had.

I'm not sure what took us to Cattaraugus, New York, but that's where it feels like my life actually began, where I began to feel alive. I was about nine years old. Cattaraugus was a small town—not more than a thousand people—and a homey place to live. There was a deli that sold pizzas, a bar that had a cigarette machine, a Methodist church, a small grocery store, and a bank. My family moved several times within this small town, but we lived there for about three years, which was a long time for us. I don't know that we'd ever lived in one town or one home for a full school year before that, much less an actual full year. So in my limited understanding of life, I felt settled in Cattaraugus. I had friends. We had other family members near us. I played baseball, rode bikes, and lived life like a normal kid. Well, what I considered normal.

My mother worked a lot—usually the swing shift—so by the time my sister and I walked home from school, she was gone. We would be asleep long before she got home. We had free rein, though by now Mandy—three years older—no longer wanted me tagging along. This was when my friends, Tom and Tonya, and I started stealing cigarettes from their parents. We thought we were so cool. Their parents both smoked a lot and didn't notice the disappearing cigarettes, except for the one time we got busted. They also drank beer, and Tonya snuck us a beer a time or two. I hated the taste, so I would pretend to drink until she managed to get it all down.

I wasn't always getting into trouble. Often I ran around town with my cousins, staying outside until dark and going to Aunt Marian's house. I don't think she was actually my aunt, and if she was, she had to have been my great-aunt, but in any case, her house was always open. The doors were never locked, and she never told me that I'd have to leave or come some other time. Her husband, Uncle Ace, was the kindest, gentlest man I have ever known. He played the harmonica. At their house, I was loved and wanted. Aunt Marian was always baking homemade bread and would let me help her. I can still smell the fresh-baked yumminess.

My great-grandma Bartlett also lived nearby. She was nice but not fun. I only visited her house if I was sick and couldn't go to school. Staying with her wasn't worth faking an illness! Besides, I loved school, though I struggled academically.

Hunting for Home

In fourth grade, I was in band, and one day the band teacher printed out a roll sheet for an upcoming program. My last name was White, the last name on the list. He ran out of room, and so to fit all the names on one sheet of paper, he shortened my name to B. J. White. Up to this point, everyone had always called me by my full name, Billy Jo. Never just Billy. Always Billy Jo.

Needless to say, it stuck. It was a welcome change. I had been teased my whole life for having a boy's name, and now finally my name was just initials. Somehow this was better, but I would eventually learn that kids would find a way to be cruel sooner or later.

By the end of fifth grade, I had fallen so far behind academically that I either failed or my mother held me back. I think they allowed your parents the choice to hold you back instead of failing you, as if it really made a difference. This was difficult for me socially, because all my friends had been promoted to the next grade.

A year later my father came back into our lives. In the years since he'd left, we'd only had an occasional phone call and one short visit over a school holiday—but he'd spent most of that with his girlfriend. He never sent any gifts or money; probably didn't trust my mother to actually use it to care for me. But still, I craved to have him in my life.

My father lived in Texas, and my parents decided that I would spend the entire summer alone with him, and then Mandy and my mother would join us in time for school. I was excited—it would be just like when we'd lived in the pink motel. My dream was finally coming true. Yes, I would miss my friends, but I would have my dad.

I flew to Tyler, Texas, on June 27, his birthday. The date was significant because, in my mind, arriving on his birthday made me his gift. Gifts were wanted. After all these years, he wanted me!

Chapter 3

Dirty

When I boarded the plane in New York, I was 100 percent Yankee. Then I met this beautiful airline assistant who had a distinct southern drawl, and I was absolutely enthralled with her. She even gave me a Dallas Cowboys cheerleader leather jacket! By the time I landed in Tyler, Texas, I had her "sound" down, along with a new vocabulary, which included *yee-haw* and *y'all*. With this new twang, I could pass for a true country-girl Texan.

The summer heat made it too hot to wear my new jacket, so I slung it over my arm and headed for the exit, scanning the crowd for my dad. His tall, skinny frame wasn't difficult to spot in the small lobby. He stood leaning against a wall, waiting, with a cigarette hanging from his lips, his hair slicked back. I raised a hand to catch his eye, excited yet nervous to see my dad again for the first time in so many years. He saw me, and when he came over, he actually had tears in his eyes. *He's glad I'm here!*

"Look how grown-up you are, Billy Jo," he said, taking my suitcase and giving me an awkward hug.

"I'm almost thirteen," I responded.

The first weeks of living in Texas, we went to the movies and out to eat all the time. But my fairy tale was short lived. Soon strange things started happening. We had a small mobile home, and I slept in the same bed with my father. One night I woke because of movement in the bed. *What is he doing?* I knew it wasn't right, but I wasn't sure why or how. I felt uncomfortable, and yet . . . I was curious. What was that gross smell mingled with his sweat? He eventually got up and left the room, and I drifted back to sleep. This nighttime ritual began happening more frequently, until one night, he touched me. And then he took my hand to touch himself. I laid still, trying to keep my breathing even so he wouldn't know I was awake. I wanted to be wanted, but not like this. This was nasty and made me feel gross.

Life only got worse after Mandy and my mother moved in. I no longer slept in the same bed as my father—my mother now filled that space. Though our sleeping arrangements were altered, the secrets after dark continued, with my father coming to my room after my mother was asleep. We didn't go to church anymore. My father hated the church and anything to do with God. Now that Mandy and I were older, Mom was no longer able to parade me in to beg for help. I'd thought that having my parents back together would be a good thing, but they did nothing but fight.

My mother was infatuated with my father, but he seemed to hate her. Her love for him was simply a weapon he could use against her. He was always criticizing her and pointing out her every flaw—her size, her smell, her cooking, her clothes. This wasn't the father I remembered. He was vulgar, cussing and drinking and telling dirty jokes.

One day, he came home drunk and spat these words at me: "I don't want you. I wish you'd never been born."

That day I died inside. My father didn't want me. This was worse than not knowing if there was going to be dinner that day. Worse than having to make up pretend Christmas gifts to talk about with my friends. I hated my mother for keeping me from him most of my life. I hated her for making him turn into a monster. I hated her for every reason imaginable. But I couldn't blame her for him not wanting me. Instead, I turned the hatred toward myself. I hated my life. I was a broken, angry, scared, starved-for-attention shell of a girl.

I spent sixth grade in a primarily black school. For a dorky white kid from upstate New York with worn-out clothes, tacky shoes, and a name like Billy Jo, this was a culture shock for me. I didn't fit in, to say the least. I had a target on my back for bullies and mean kids. They teased me nearly nonstop. The popular kids rammed me into the lockers, made fun of my name, and started cruel, sexually inspired jokes. I was the laughingstock of school that year.

I was scared to go to school every day. I was scared to go home every day. I had no safe place.

One weekend we went to visit Aunt Lee and Uncle Benny. My parents stayed at the house to visit and sent me off to the city pool with some other friends and relatives. I swam with one of the other girls, and her father stuck around to keep an eye on us. But he did more than that. He pulled me into his lap and put his fingers inside my bathing suit.

"Better sit still or people will know what a bad little girl you are," he whispered.

Panic rose inside my chest. The others were too far away to notice. I felt so gross, so alone, so violated. This was worse than my father touching me. I desperately wanted my father's approval, but this man? I wanted nothing from him. *Why doesn't someone stop this? Doesn't anyone see how scared I am?*

"Don't tell anyone about this," he warned. "No one will believe a trashy girl like you."

When I left that day, I was forever a different girl. I believed him and kept this disgusting little secret for several months before telling my parents. When I finally worked up the courage, I approached them one evening as they sat on the pull-out sofa that also served as their bed.

"Can I talk to you about something?"

"What is it?" my father asked.

I stared at the floor and started my story. I tried to tell them everything, but my father cut me off.

"Stop lying. Slim is a dear family friend and would never have done such a thing. If he did, it must have been because you wanted him to, and you should not have allowed that to happen. Promise me you won't mention this again."

I hadn't known what to expect, but it wasn't this. I'd been fearful but hopeful that I might receive some comfort, love, or genuine tenderness. I'd longed for some type of understanding or affirmation. But their response was, if possible, more painful than the molestation. Maybe my father was trying to hide his own perverse secret. I shut down completely and fled the room.

Were all men disgusting pigs? What was it about me that attracted these vile men? Could they tell by looking at me that I had no one to protect me? Maybe word got around that I was a filthy little girl. Or maybe all my friends just had fathers like mine. At one friend's house, her father regularly exposed himself while I was around. At another friend's house, her father, Stanley, started brushing against me and squeezed my chest when he lifted me onto the trampoline. I was repulsed. I didn't want to go back there after that, but my mother encouraged me to be friends with his daughter.

One day when I came home from school, my mother met me at the door.

"Our neighbor Stanley wants you to do some yard work for him while his family is gone this weekend. He'll pay you."

I stiffened; red flags raised.

"No, I don't want to be around him, especially not alone. He gives me the creeps!"

I didn't tell her about the touching. Why would I? I'd learned from the last time that if I told, it would only cause more hurt.

"Billy Jo, we need the money. I'll go with you, and I won't leave you alone."

Dirty

I consented reluctantly. "All right. You promise not to leave me alone?"

"I promise."

When we arrived at Stanley's house, he seemed peeved that my mother remained. He stationed her in the front yard in a lawn chair while I raked leaves in the back. Every once in a while, he came back to "check" on me, which always involved an unwanted hug.

"Keep raking. I'll be right back," he said.

After he left, I paused, put my rake aside, and walked around the side of the house. From there, I could see my mother get into his car. He loaded several brown bags of groceries into the trunk and then climbed into the driver's seat to take her home. I couldn't stop the tears that trickled down my cheeks as I watched them drive away. She was leaving me here . . . alone.

When he got back, he called to me.

"You're working too hard. Come inside for a drink."

I didn't want a drink. I wanted a mother to protect me. I wanted to go home. I wanted to be loved. But I had no choice except to follow him into the house. As he brought me a glass of lemonade, I noticed him lock the door, and my heart started racing. He walked into another room, still talking, but my ears muffled his words as I watched him unbutton his shirt, gross old-man chest hair spilling out. The second he turned his back, I bolted—out the door, up the street, all the way home. By the time I reached our house, I was in a full-blown rage. I rarely expressed my emotions. It was safer to keep my hurt and shame and fear bottled up. But now every ounce of fury and resentment came gushing out.

My mother looked up as I burst into the room.

"You left me!" I yelled, swearing at her. "You promised not to leave. You promised!"

This betrayal—there was nothing like it. *How could she have left me? Did she really not care?* She didn't know about my father touching me. With Slim, maybe she couldn't bring herself to believe it. But this time, I had forewarned her. This time she knew. *She knew.* Yet she'd still left me there.

She sat silent, never responding, never denying. Just sat. A few tears fell from her own eyes as I cried hysterically. Maybe she was stunned?

I hated her with all that I was, yet hate was too mild a word for what I felt. She had traded me for frozen food. I could never forgive her.

Chapter 4

Looking for Love

By seventh grade, I was a different girl. Hardened. Seasoned. That summer I made friends with some older girls on my street. They started telling me I should wear more makeup. Fix my hair. Loosen up some. I adopted an attitude, and my new friends opened the door to popularity that I had only dreamed of. I was cool. Wanted. For the first time ever, I was in the "in" crowd, which really was the rough crowd. There were a lot of us. Hurting. Lonely. Hungry. The good kids wanted nothing to do with me. Nice kids with nice homes and nice families didn't associate with kids like me. The bad crowd—that group took me in. They accepted me the way I was—broken. They "loved" me through my pain. They understood the need to numb myself—usually by getting high or drunk. I finally had something to fill those hurting voids in my life.

Instead of worrying about not having nice clothes, I started cutting my old, worn-out ones to create my own style. Jeans too small? Cut them into short shorts—tight, too-small-for-your-behind shorts! Boys liked that. The boys started to show me lots of attention—attention I desperately craved. I didn't get the love I sought at home, so I looked for it elsewhere. Someone. Anyone. I needed to be loved so badly—not sexually, but just to be wanted by those who are supposed to naturally want you.

There was one boy in particular, Cruz, that I was crazy about. He was in high school and had dark hair and chiseled features—a total hunk! One day he came over to my house after school, and we began messing around in my bed. We were fully clothed, but some major romance was in the air. Or at least it was, until my father walked in on us.

"Get out," he said, showing Cruz the door.

"Dad," I protested. "Please let him stay." My dad had made it clear he didn't want me, other than for sick reasons, so why did he have to kick out this awesome guy who did?

After Cruz made a quick exit, my father motioned to me.

"Come with me."

I followed him into the living room, heartbroken and embarrassed and angry. He sat on the couch and patted the cushion next to him. I pouted and sat down.

"I need to warn you about what boys want," he said.

Oh, I was feeling warned all right. And for good reason. My father's "warning" involved teaching me what boys had and the consequences of touching them in certain ways—by personal demonstration. Right in the broad daylight of our living room. This was very bad. Bad to do. Bad to let those boys do . . . yet apparently okay for him to show to me. This was the first time he was openly inappropriate with me. But by this point, I was pretty immune to the pain caused by this kind of treatment.

That last bit was actually true—I was looking for attention. Because my parents did not supervise us, my friends and I had free rein to do what we wanted. I often snuck out of my bedroom window at night to go party, almost hoping to be caught. I actually was caught a time or two, but my mom didn't care. I really had no need to sneak out. I could have freely walked out the front door. Still, I would sneak out, party, climb back in my window. Start the next day, silently screaming for someone to care. To see. How could so many people see me but not actually see?

My crowd often went to an old well in the middle of nowhere and played loud music, smoked pot, drank beer we bought illegally, and of course, made out. I had no problems making out with these guys. After all, they "loved me." I was so lonely and hungry for approval that I believed their lies. I was hot, fun, and willing, so I got around. I somehow remained a virgin, only because I was terrified of doing it wrong or of my body not working like a normal girl's bodies should. But I did just about everything else. My innocence was long gone.

I'd already had my heart broken a few times when I met Andy. He had no job, no car, and no ambition, but he was so nice to me—acted like he wanted to give me the world. He did courteous little things like saying please and thank you, getting me a drink of water or iced tea, baking me a frozen pizza. I'd never experienced someone showing me affection or loving consideration. I thought he was a great catch.

He had a rare 1965 Ford Falcon two-door hardtop with no motor, sitting on blocks in his yard, waiting to be restored by a father obsessed with muscle cars and easy women. His father, Larry—a mechanic— was always promising to get it running for him, but to the best of my knowledge, it never left that yard. Andy and I would sit in that old broken-down hunk of junk and dream up our future.

"What do you want for your life, Andy?" I asked one night as we sat on the leather seats, going nowhere.

"Someday I'm gonna buy you a big house, and we'll have a fancy car like this one. And my dad, he'll be so proud of me." He ran a hand through his long dark hair.

"I'd be happy with any home that I lived in more than a few months. Someday I want to have a career and be a mom. I want to be somebody." *Somebody who was wanted and loved.*

"Maybe we'll run away together. Live happily ever after," Andy said, and we passed a joint back and forth. Our dreams became more of a dazed stare. "Wanna make out?"

There was only one problem with our big dreams: my dad forbade me to see Andy. *Like he had the right to tell me who I could and couldn't date!* In my opinion, it was a little late for him to become the concerned parent. His opposition, of course, only made Andy more attractive to me. I decided to act on the dream of running away.

I felt an intense need to get away. To run. I didn't want to ever stop running. So about four in the morning, I got up, threw a handful of clothes in a bag, and ran. All the hurt, the drama, the craziness of my life had reached a massive boiling point, so I ran to the only person who I thought might protect me. Not to Andy—but Andy's mother, Jackie.

When every person in my life was emotionally removed from my heart, she was there. She knew enough about my home life to know I needed an escape. Jackie was the opposite of my mother. Though she was also a large woman, she was always well kept. She put on makeup, bathed regularly, and always wore earrings—two in each ear. She took pristine care of everything else too. Her beloved pearl-white 1964 Ford Galaxy was spotless. Her single-wide mobile home was immaculate. Everything had a place. You needed Tylenol? It was on the third shelf, two over from the left. Scissors? Kitchen, top drawer by the stove on the right side.

Jackie was kind, welcoming, and compassionate. She was a mom. Not a perfect mom, but a mom. She tried hard to show her family love, to provide for them, and to care for them. She washed clothes and cooked meals and did the dishes. We would play games and paint our toenails, talk, and laugh. She'd even taught me how to do basic housework. They were small things, but having a woman show me how to dust or cook a decent meal that didn't come from a box made an impact on my life. She was the mother I didn't have. If I was honest, I was dating Andy mostly so I could have Jackie in my life.

I ran the whole way, all seven miles. Well, the whole way except for an unscheduled fall that skinned my hands and knees. The sun was beginning to peek through the blackness of the night when I finally arrived. Everyone was still asleep, and the house was dark and quiet. Andy's bedroom was on the closest end of their driveway. I snuck in.

"Andy, wake up!" I whispered.

He sat up and swung his legs over the side of the bed.

"BJ, is that you?" he asked, rubbing his eyes.

"Yeah, I didn't know where else to go."

He stood up, and I collapsed into his arms, exhausted from running, exhausted from life. He led me over to the closet, opened the door, and quietly pushed aside a mess of clothes.

"You can hide here until everyone leaves for work. I'll skip classes and come back home, and then we can make a plan."

I slipped in, laying my head back against the wall in the inky blackness, and he pulled the door closed. As I lay hidden in my boyfriend's closet, I felt oddly safe. Once Jackie knew I was there, she would somehow help. But my fantasy was short lived.

I must have fallen asleep, because I woke to the sound of police officers and slivers of red and blue lights flashing through the slashes of the thick blanket covering the window. Those bright lights were a stark contrast to the deep darkness that mirrored my heart. *God, if you're there, please don't let them find me! I can't go back home.* This was not how this was supposed to be unfolding. I was supposed to stay hidden all day, and when Jackie came home from work, Andy would explain how I needed protection and a place to stay, and she would lovingly doctor my skinned hands and knees and decide I could stay. I would be loved and safe. Instead, my heart pounded so heavily, I was sure they could hear it outside.

I wasn't sure if Jackie hadn't yet left for work or if she'd been called home by the police, but I heard her speaking with a policeman at the front door.

"Ma'am, we have reason to believe you are harboring a runaway minor. We'd like to search your home."

There was a scuffle of footsteps as she let them in. As much as I wanted asylum, I couldn't let this woman I adored get into trouble for me. She didn't know I was here hiding, and I couldn't let her take the blame. She was kind and loving, and this wasn't her fault. I deserved any consequences of my attempted escape, not her. Before the police could find me, I slithered out into the open and nonchalantly walked down the hallway toward the commotion and toward my fate.

They called my mother as soon as I appeared. While she was on her way, an officer interrogated me.

"We were at your house and discovered several entries you wrote in your diary about sexual abuse. Are those accusations true?"

I looked up at him. His expression was so stern and intimidating. When I didn't answer, he went on.

"Those are very damaging accusations you've made, young lady, and if they aren't true, you need to confess. Otherwise, we'll be conducting an investigation."

I didn't want my father to get in trouble, and I didn't trust that justice would be served anyway. What difference would it make if anyone did believe me? I'd just get another lecture on how I caused those men to do these things. I would be the one on trial, not them. It would be easier and less painful to say I'd made it all up. My dad had never touched me inappropriately. Slim had never touched me. Neighbor man Stanley had never made a move. I was looking for attention, that's all. I vehemently denied the truth, just wanting this day to end.

Chapter 5

Two Little Girls

I knew Andy was home when the front door slammed—never a good sign. He appeared in the kitchen a few minutes later, wearing a favorite black T-shirt emblazoned with a heavy-metal band graphic, probably Metallica or Megadeth. It hung loosely on his lanky frame.

"I'm hungry. Did you make any food?" he said, barely looking at me.

I nodded toward the oven. "I think the pizza is done."

He yanked open the oven door and pulled it out. "You burned it! How hard is it to follow the directions on the box?"

I shrank back against the counter. "You saw your dad today, didn't you." It was more of a statement than a question. He just grunted. His dad had probably chewed him out for something.

Andy, always frustrated that he could not measure up to his father's expectations or earn his love and approval, usually took his disappointment out on me. In the beginning, he had been smitten with me, like I was a prize he had won. Now, he had become emotionally absent, controlling, and just plain mean.

I cut the pizza into slices. For a few minutes, silence hung between us, until Andy finally looked at me, scanning up and down.

"Why do you do your hair like that? It's not attractive. Maybe if you put as much effort into your hair as you do your makeup, you'd have a chance of not looking ugly."

I pushed a strand behind my ear self-consciously. I thought my ponytail looked fine, but I wanted to please him. "I could braid it tomorrow. Would you like that?"

He shrugged.

"I'll be in our room."

My parents had called it quits again, and Mandy and I were on our own with my mother. With my father out of the way, boys were allowed to spend the night, and she had even let Andy move in with us. She gave him a place to stay, and I gave him my virginity.

Considering the way men had treated me, I thought Andy was the best I deserved. He might have been an angry, no-ambition jerk, but he loved me. And he told me often. Those three little words were powerful and manipulative to this starved-for-affection girl.

Around the time things started to go south with Andy, Mandy, now seventeen, got pregnant. She was excited, and so was everybody around us. As I watched her being pampered and coddled and encouraged, I hatched a genius plan. Since Andy and I were sexually active now, I would tell him that I was expecting too! Of course, he would be so excited that he would magically morph into some kind of super boyfriend, take care of me, grow some ambition, and put some action behind his endless dreams. Then in a couple of months, I would "miscarry." Naturally, out of remorse and compassion, he would continue to love and pamper me, keep his ambition, and we would live happily ever after. What a plan!

It was foolproof . . . at first. When I told Andy I was pregnant, he did change his behavior toward me. But the special treatment was short lived because each time we broke up and got back together, his behavior became more abusive. I was ready to end the farce but had to face a shocking reality: the pretend pregnancy wasn't so make-believe after all. I really was pregnant. Fourteen years old, seventh grade, getting high daily, loser boyfriend, and expecting a child.

I didn't tell anyone for five months. For my first trimester, the buzz was all about Mandy having a baby. No one paid any mind to what I was doing or ever talked about the possibility of me being pregnant, until one day at the gas station.

I rolled out of the passenger seat and walked around to the pump, while my mother went inside to pay. By the time she came back out, I was crying.

She looked at me. "Are you pregnant?"

We hadn't been talking about anything, but she must have been suspicious, and I knew I needed to tell her.

I nodded yes, pulling the pump lever to start the flow of fuel while trying to stop the flow of tears.

She didn't say anything. She just turned and walked back into the gas station for change. That was the only time she ever mentioned my pregnancy. It soon became clear that while Mandy's pregnancy was celebrated, mine was a disappointment. Mandy didn't speak to me for a while after she found out. She probably felt like I got pregnant to steal her moment. She didn't have to be jealous though, because Mom focused all her excitement on her first child and first grandchild. Only Jackie showed any excitement for me and my baby. My mother had long since abdicated that role to her.

It wasn't Jackie's ideal plan to become such a young grandmother, but she loved me and supported me anyway. I think she felt sorry for me, though she never let on about it. Jackie had been a young mom herself. She'd had Andy when she was eighteen and had stayed in an unhappy marriage with his cheating father for many long years. I got the sense that she wanted more for me than what she'd had. Jackie didn't really approve of my relationship with her son—not because she disapproved of me, but because she recognized that our relationship was too serious, too soon. She was also concerned with the way Andy imitated his father's unhealthy behavior when he belittled me or flew into a rage over the smallest of conflicts. Still, she'd given us the wedding rings that had belonged to her and Andy's father.

Andy sometimes joked that the rings were tainted with bad luck since their marriage was such a disaster, but for me it was like getting a special family heirloom passed down from a greatly loved and admired woman. I focused more on who had worn the ring than the symbolism of the failed marriage. We wore the rings even though we weren't married yet. And now we had a baby on the way.

I had no more business having a baby than the man in the moon, but something happened inside of me when I found out I was expecting—something profound. I knew I did not want my baby living the same life I had lived. I knew I wanted my baby to be loved and to feel loved every day of her life. I would die proving to the world that I could be a great mom. I was instantly in love with my baby. No one ever suggested adoption or abortion. I didn't even know what abortion was.

I still had a crazy home life. Still had a crappy boyfriend. I had to switch to a school for pregnant teens. But I was going to be a mother. Me . . . a mother. I immediately stopped smoking cigarettes and pot. I had never been much on nutrition, but I tried to eat healthier and to take care of myself, though I did eat a lot of pizza and chocolate peanut butter cups during the remainder of the nine months. I got huge! I gained sixty pounds and a condition called toxemia, or preeclampsia. It causes severe complications, including hypertension and swelling, especially in very young mothers-to-be. I was so swollen. Ankles to knees the same thickness. Hands and fingers like fat sausages. Face fat and puffy. Even my eyes were swollen.

Mandy and I gave birth within a week of each other, to daughters. She delivered my niece on my due date, the day before my fifteenth birthday. For obvious reasons, there was not much of a birthday bash the next day for me, though that was pretty normal. Six days later, my little girl made her debut. I was in labor for about thirty-six hours.

They had to stop my contractions at one point to treat the toxemia and then restart labor using induction medication. When I went into the hospital, my ring would not even go on my finger. By the evening after my daughter was born, my ring would not stay on my finger. Turns out that a large portion of my weight gain was fluid.

I named her Ashlei. When the nurse placed her in my arms, I felt a love so genuine, so complete, that the awe of it overwhelmed me. This tiny hairy human was my child! In an instant I was determined to protect her and to make sure she felt a mother's love so her life would be different than mine. I imagined making her breakfast, fixing her a plate of food, braiding her hair—none of the things a newborn baby would need, but all things I thought described a good mother.

At the same time, I felt a staggering fear of failing motherhood. How was I going to do this? My thoughts bounced frantically between my happily-ever-after fairy-tale dreams to the dark reality of being fifteen, uneducated, and alone. Sure, I had Andy, but who knew how long he would stick around? I knew deep down that I would be the one responsible to protect and provide for her.

I went back to school just a couple of weeks after Ashlei was born. I had every intention of finishing school, going to college, and making a great life for me and my daughter. Despite my past academic challenges, I had grown to love learning. But there were consequences to my choices. Middle school was way different as a mother. All the other kids were going to football games and school dances; I went home to care for my baby. Not that I knew what I was doing. I didn't breastfeed. The thought of a baby doing that to me was disgusting! No way was I going to have a baby on my breast. When she was old enough to eat solids, I wouldn't feed her anything I thought was gross. I didn't like green beans, so why on earth would I ever make my baby girl eat that nasty stuff? Peas? Ick! No way.

At first I thought I could do it all—be a mom, go to school, get good grades, still be a kid myself, and play house. But soon I had to choose between taking care of my baby or doing homework. There were endless diapers, laundry, diapers, spit-up, colic-filled crying nights, diapers, fevers, teething, and did I mention diapers? Plus, I had to sleep somewhere in there. My family helped as much as they could with Ash so I could remain in school, but it was just too hard. And too expensive. Diapers weren't free, and neither was formula or baby food or baby clothes.

My baby wasn't fatherless, but Andy, three years older than me and only eighteen, wasn't much on the whole supporting-our-family idea. He didn't work, he didn't have a car, he didn't have a home—but he was there. Mostly because he had nowhere else to go. High school dropout that couldn't pass a drug test didn't look good on job applications. Shocker, right?

Somehow I finished the eighth grade, but how on earth would I manage high school? My dreams seemed further and further from reality.

Chapter 6

Red Flags and Regrets

The day of my wedding did not go off exactly as planned. It was a mess. Jackie, my mom, and Andy's stepmother had gathered in the bridal room of the church to help me get ready for the big moment.

"You look beautiful," Jackie whispered, giving my shoulders a squeeze. Her seamstress friend had made the white gown I now wore.

"Thanks," I said.

My mother's gift had been to sign for me to get married, as I was still underage. It was like being legally set free from my home. I was more excited about that than about getting married.

We all turned at a knock at the door.

"I've got it," I said, crossing the room and cracking the door enough to see who was on the other side. It was the pastor. We hadn't met previously. He had agreed over the phone to marry us. He hadn't inquired about our relationship with God; nor had he offered marital counseling. He was available and we could afford his budget price, so we'd set the date.

"Hi. What is it?" I asked, holding the door awkwardly between us.

He leaned in discreetly. "Honey . . . I just met your groom. I can wait three or four weeks to send in the marriage license if you would like. You know, in case you change your mind."

What, him too? Last night my bridesmaid had bailed, telling me that she couldn't stand with me knowing what a mistake I was making. I wanted to tell the pastor yes, please wait. I secretly hoped he would insist. Instead, I giggled to cover up my shame, embarrassment, and nagging feelings of doubt.

"No, I'm sure. I have to do this. It's best for our daughter to have married parents."

He nodded his head and stepped back. "Okay. Then we're ready for you."

I was not in love with Andy, but I thought marrying him was the best thing for Ashlei. I thought two married parents living together would give her the love and security I had always longed for. My vows that day were a necessary commitment to ensure a happy, safe life for her. I would keep my promise to make sure she wouldn't have the same life I had been given. I refused to call off the wedding, because I was afraid of raising Ashlei alone—and I was afraid of losing Jackie too.

I allowed myself a smile as I watched eleven-month-old Ashlei toddle down the aisle in front of me. I had a small bouquet, but the church was otherwise devoid of decorations. There were not many people in attendance—his family, as most of mine had refused to come. But my father had come to walk me down the aisle. In a matter of minutes, it was all over.

We had a small reception with a homemade cake, punch, and chips. I changed out of my wedding gown into a blue pencil skirt and blouse, and off we rode to our honeymoon. While Ashlei stayed with Jackie and her husband, Ed, we ate dinner at a local restaurant and spent the night in a motel not far from our new apartment. Awkward silence filled the evening. The only memorable part of the night was the pranks Jackie had prepared in our room, like plastic wrap lining the toilet bowl and petroleum jelly on the toilet seat. We scavenged the room, looking for all the booby traps. Andy was not impressed. In the end, we just rolled a joint, laid back on the uncomfortable motel bed, got high, and went to sleep. Some honeymoon.

Life as husband and wife was about the same as it had been before. I finally had my own home, but this was no fairy-tale ending. Andy still wouldn't work, and many nights he didn't even come home. The responsibility of paying our rent and bills fell to me, so I went to work for a hamburger joint. At that time in the state of Texas, you had to be at least sixteen to get a job, so I lied about my age. I doubt my new boss believed whatever age I told him I was, but he didn't let on. Maybe he recognized my predicament, because he was kind to me. Often, he let me clock back in to get extra hours during my split shift. I worked hard for him, and he valued me for it.

When you either work or watch your baby go without diapers, you work hard. We didn't have a car, so I walked the five miles to work, often with Ashlei in tow because Andy hadn't come home in time to watch her. Sometimes Jackie and Ed showed up "just to eat," and would take her for the day. Other times they would come for dinner near closing and graciously wait for me to get off so they could give me a ride home. They weren't proud of the way Andy had turned out, so they did what they could to help me.

If Andy showed up at my work to pick up Ashlei, he made sure everyone knew what a lousy human being I was.

"Why do you let him talk to you that way?" my coworker Kristi asked. "He treats you like you don't deserve any courtesy or respect." The way Andy treated me was evident to everyone, and I hated him for it. Still, I had an answer.

"I can't leave him. Because of Ashlei. It's not really that bad." But it was. Andy pointed out my every flaw. He insisted on knowing my every move. If I was even five minutes late, he accused me of sleeping around. If I cooked eggs for breakfast, he wanted oatmeal. I couldn't have an opinion on anything, and nothing I did was ever good enough.

Kristi didn't look like she believed me, but she let it drop and changed the subject.

"Hey, do you want to go to church with me sometime?"

Kristi talked about her church often and the times she sang with the choir. I hadn't been to church in years, but other than my mom using me to get food and money there, I had positive memories. I'd been feeling like something was missing in my life. Maybe this was it.

"Yeah, I'd like that." *Wait, what am I thinking?* Doubts and insecurities began to take over. "Wait, I don't know. I don't have a way to get there. I don't even own a dress."

Kristi was undeterred. "Oh, that's no problem. My mom and I will pick you up, and I have a dress you can borrow. My mom can even do your hair."

"All right, then I guess I can go."

On Sunday morning, my body bubbled with excitement as I styled my freshly permed hair and applied some of the makeup Kristi had lent me. I hadn't felt this nice in a long time. This happy. I glanced at the clock on the wall. They would be here any minute. I heard someone at the door, but it wasn't Kristi; it was Andy, home after another night out partying. He stopped in his tracks as he came into the bedroom and saw me.

"Why are you dressed up?" he demanded, eyes narrowing.

"A friend invited me to go to church," I said, smoothing out a wrinkle in the dress.

"I don't believe you. You haven't been to church in years. Are you cheating on me?"

I was familiar with Andy's jealousy and suspicion. In his mind, there was no reason for me to get all dressed up unless it was for another man. I heard a honk from the road.

"That's them," I said, heading for the door. Andy stepped in front of me, blocking the doorway.

"You're leaving me, aren't you?" he accused, slamming the doorframe with the palm of his hand, already well on his way into a rage.

"No! Like I said, I'm going to church."

Kristi knocked on our door, oblivious to World War III happening inside our home. Andy refused to let me answer it or leave. I would not be going to church today. Tears streaked mascara down my face as

I watched them drive away without me.

My friendship with Kristi deteriorated after that humiliating Sunday. So did my resolve to stay with Andy. Having a job where I not only earned a living but received daily validation about being a good mom and a dependable hard worker gave me a sense of independence. When my coworkers kept telling me I could do much better than Andy, I started to believe them. Maybe being alone *would* be better than taking care of him and putting up with his emotional and verbal abuse.

As broken as I was, I wasn't stupid. The harder I worked, the less my husband did. He was mean and selfish. He was losing his grasp on me, but instead of wooing me, he kept tightening his grip and berating me at every turn. Eventually I had enough and realized that he was bringing nothing into our home but heartache. Andy had always accused me of leaving him, but in the end, I asked *him* to leave.

Life without Andy was just as hard. I fell behind on paying my utility bill, and the month came when they were going to shut off my electricity. I did the only thing I could think of—I called my mother. I had to admit that as a single mother, she had always managed to scrounge what we needed, even in dire circumstances. I gritted my teeth and made the call. She told me to go to her church, telling me what to say so the pastor would pay my bill. *No, anything but that!* I'd sworn that I would never ask a church for help, never be like my mother. But what other option did I have?

I went in, hating myself more than anything, only to discover the pastor shared that sentiment. He verbally attacked me, throwing around words like "prostitute" and "whore" because "that's what Scripture called unwed mothers." As if I weren't already humiliated enough having to beg for help. Technically, I was still married, just not living with my husband—but that didn't seem to count in his book. I wouldn't take it.

"Fine, keep your stupid God money!" I shouted, spitting a curse at him.

I never wanted to enter a church again.

Chapter 7

More Broken

"BJ, there's this guy here you should meet." Mandy wiped the countertop from behind the bar as I sipped on a soda at the pizza place where she worked.

"Here, now?" I hadn't exactly made the best decisions about men since breaking up with Andy, but Mandy had been persistent in trying to set me up.

"Yeah. He's a cook, working in the back. He's going on break now. You want to meet him?"

"Okay."

A few minutes later, a stocky teen walked out to where we were. He wasn't tall, but he was taller than me, with crystal-blue eyes and a dimple in his cheek. He stuck out his hand.

"Hi, I'm Joe."

"BJ. Nice to meet you."

Joe wasn't really my type, but he was flirty and made me laugh. More importantly, he had a job and a house and a car. When he picked me up for our first date in his red T-top Camaro, I was hooked. We started going steady, and he gave me rides to work. That sure beat walking! He showered me with gifts and compliments, like Andy used to. He told me often that I was beautiful. Who didn't love to feel beautiful and desired? And he was great with Ashlei. However, his mother was not a huge fan of mine. She was no Jackie. In fact, the first Christmas I spent with them, she actually hung his old girlfriend's stocking up for me! She'd crossed the old name out and written my name in black sharpie beneath it.

I was undeterred. Again, I thought I was in love. Again, we went too serious, too soon. Ashlei and I moved in with Joe. As soon as he turned eighteen, he landed a job at a local company that manufactured air conditioners and paid well, considering his age. We had what I thought was a terrific life—better than anything I'd ever known growing up, that's for sure. Which was why, when I found out I was pregnant again, I was giddy at the thought of having his baby. Despite the challenges I'd faced, more than anything I loved being a mom. And we'd already been together for a year and a half.

"I have some news," I told Joe when he came home from work. I could barely contain my smile.

"Yeah?" He bent down beside our rumpled king-sized bed to take off his shoes.

"I'm pregnant!"

Joe looked up, frozen, his shoe still in hand. The air went cold between us. I felt my heart stop at the look on his face.

"I don't want to be a father."

"What?" I whispered. This was not what I had expected. In an instant, my excitement turned to shock and devastation. Immediately, I sucked in all my emotion.

"How far along are you?" he asked.

"Four weeks. I just found out."

"I don't want you to have that baby."

My father's drunken words came back to me. *I wish you had never been born.* They hurt as much now as they had then. Many times in my childhood I, too, had wished that I had never been born. All I could think was that I would never let an unwanted child be born into what

I had been born into. I could not—I would not—bring this baby into a home where he or she was not wanted, plain and simple.

"Okay," I said. "I'll make an appointment for an abortion."

He didn't respond.

Two weeks later, we drove to Dallas, went into the clinic, and paid our fee. There was a law that women had to be counseled before they could go through with an abortion. My "counseling" consisted of me crying, begging permission to keep my baby, and the counselor insisting that I was making the right decision. How horrible to even consider bringing this unwanted baby into the world. I bought that lie, signed on the dotted line, and followed her back to the procedure room. No privacy. The nurse tossed me a hospital gown.

"Change into this and lie down."

I slipped out of my clothes, pulled the blue fabric over my shoulders, and lay back on the uncomfortable medical table. The nurse gave me some medication.

"This will help you relax."

A doctor came in.

"Close your eyes, and it will be over soon. You'll feel a little pressure, but in a day or two you'll be as good as new."

The next few minutes seemed unending as my unborn child was literally sucked from my body. I cried through the entire procedure. Joe might not have wanted this baby, but I did. I was heartbroken. Truly, a part of me died that day.

After it was over, I got dressed, and the nurse gave me some antibiotics to prevent infection and some pain medication.

"You're free to leave," she said.

In less than an hour, I had been counseled, aborted my child, and was now on my way home. All I could do was sit in silence in the car with tears streaming down my face. Joe didn't say anything. This man, who just days ago I could not have imagined loving more, I now hated. I hated him for not loving our child. I hated him for wanting me to take our child's life. I hated him for letting me take our child's life—for not stopping me, for not protecting me, for not protecting our baby. I just felt empty. Completely empty.

We stopped at a fast-food place on our way home, and I don't know if I even took one bite, but my soul, did I feel sick! I spent the next thirty minutes in the bathroom, throwing up and crying as the full realization of what I had done began to surface. There were no take-backs in the abortion world. Already that "quick fix" was turning into a lifelong wound, never to be forgotten. Joe and I did not talk about the details of that day or of the child who was lost.

The next year was a blur. I went through a major depression, gained another person's worth of weight, and eventually became obsessed with getting pregnant again. I was sure that if I just had another baby, it would make everything better. I was not trying to replace the baby I had aborted, nor did I think I would have that same baby, but I did think that if I had *another* baby, the emptiness and pain would go away. But it was a full year before I was able to conceive again. With each month that went by, I began to think God was punishing me for killing my baby. Why would He give me another baby when I had so carelessly murdered the last one?

I was very much trying to get pregnant again, and Joe knew it. We didn't have any discussions about having another child, but I guess he got tired of me crying over the child we had killed and just accepted it was going to happen. But I could feel him withdrawing emotionally from our relationship. He became cold and started drinking more and more. He began working extra hours "to be able to provide for a child."

It only got worse once I was pregnant again. Anytime I complained about him working late or not coming home, he justified it by saying it was my fault he had to work more to provide for the child I'd insisted on having. In a way, he was punishing me for getting pregnant.

When I was five months pregnant, I spent one night with my sister and took Ashlei to preschool before returning home the next morning. A car that I had seen around a few times recently sat in our driveway. *That's odd.* I dismissed the thought until I reached the front door and found it locked. We never locked our door, so I didn't have a key with me. I knew instantly something bad was going on. I banged on the door for several minutes, but there was no reply. Finally I crept around the side of our house until I reached our bedroom window. I was attempting to climb in when I saw them.

Joe was in our bed with another woman.

I choked back a cry, my mind racing, my heart crumbling. *How could he do this to me?* After all I'd been through? While I was pregnant with our child?

Joe got up to stop me from coming through the window.

"Go back around front," he said, pulling on a shirt.

I stumbled back toward the front door, where he let me in. I brushed past without looking at him.

"You're acting crazy. You need to leave," he said.

I felt crazy. "Oh, I'm leaving all right. It's over. I'll be back for my things."

I moved in with Mandy. Over the next few months, I learned that Joe had been with several women while we were together. Yet even though Joe had cheated on me, I had great hopes of winning him back. I would do anything to please him. I excused his infidelity by blaming it on the stress of him becoming a father. I took all the blame for him going outside of our relationship. Clearly it was my fault.

My hopes for reconciliation were never higher than the night I gave birth to our son, Austin. Joe was by my side through the whole experience. When he left late into the night, my heart was so full. I believed he loved me. He loved our son. He would be back to see us both.

That night and all the next day, I kept hearing a strange buzzing but could not figure out what it was. It happened again while a friend sat visiting with me in the hospital room.

"Do you hear that?" I asked.

"Yeah."

She started searching and dug up a pager from the chair cushion. I recognized it as Joe's. Nine missed pages, all from the same number.

I punched the number into the hospital room phone, and after a few rings, a woman's voice said, "Hello?" I quickly hung up.

It was her.

Joe had told me he had ended things with the other woman, but he had lied. Their relationship had not ended. I felt so stupid, so betrayed, so hurt. I hadn't suspected a thing. He had been so good to me, so kind, so giving. Of course, if he kept me happy and comfortable, I would have no reason to question him . . . and I didn't.

I turned my attention to Austin to avoid the heartbreak. How I loved this precious little boy, this gift. He was so perfect, so beautiful. Somehow my broken, dead, hurting heart, full of hate and resentment, was at the same time overflowing with love and awe over this new life I had been blessed with. Now a grown-up twenty-year-old, I would do things right this time—whatever "right" was. I still wasn't sure. I knew what wrong was, and as long as I didn't repeat my own childhood for my children, that equaled success.

For this second round of motherhood, I decided to breastfeed. Some highly educated lactation consultant told me it was important to wake Austin up every couple of hours to let him nurse. Waking a sleeping baby didn't work so well! I managed to get him on a schedule of feeding every two hours and then crying for what seemed like around the clock. Eat, pee, cry. This was the first boy in my family, and every time I changed his diaper, he peed everywhere. By the end of his first month in this world, my new normal was sleep deprivation and peed-on sheets.

Ashlei took advantage of my distraction with her new baby brother. It only took a few minutes alone in a closet with her Barbies and a pair of scissors to give herself a new look. The hacks and gouges in her gorgeous long hair brought me to tears. A few days later, she did it again, and this time it wasn't repairable. She had cut chunks of hair so closely, you could see her scalp. This time I was not only devastated but frustrated. *So much for doing things right.* I was a failure as a mother.

Unfortunately, being a single mom of a newborn and a mischievous toddler wasn't enough to preoccupy me from getting revenge on the other woman. I was not typically the hold-on-to-something-forever kind of girl, but I was consumed with doing to this other woman what she had done to me, purely out of spite. When she first started sleeping with Joe, she had known I was expecting his child, and she had done it anyway. Now she was living with him in our old house.

I had lost all my depression and pregnancy weight and now made it my personal goal to get Joe to cheat on her with me. Brilliant plan, right? I knew by now that he would easily fall into bed with me or any other willing female. I fiercely wanted to hurt her, and through her, him.

All went according to plan. I went over while she was gone, slept with Joe, and left. That made me the winner, right? Wrong. Just more broken. More hurt. I was doing a fabulous job at building layers upon layers of bad decisions and adding more baggage and bondage to my emotional résumé. So much for happily ever after.

Chapter 8

The Party Begins

Pounding music thrummed through the room as I followed a silent, burly man through the crowd of people in the club toward an office in the back. I coughed on the smoky haze.

"Excuse me," I said as I bumped into some men playing pool to my right.

They looked me up and down, and I quickly moved on. The lights on stage shone out into the dark room, and a woman danced topless on center stage. *Oh my stars!* I didn't know why I was surprised. This was a gentlemen's club, after all. Not that I saw any "gentlemen" around.

The bouncer motioned toward the door to the office, still saying nothing, and I stepped inside. A woman sat behind a desk, counting stacks of bills—mostly one-dollar bills. I'd never seen so much money in my life. My friend had suggested I apply to be a waitress here. Maybe she was on to something.

The woman looked up and scanned me the same way the men had. I'd lost all that weight trying to win Joe back, so I knew I looked good. She'd never guess I had two kids at home, though that was why

I was there. Again, I found myself needing to provide diapers and food without the support of a husband.

"So you've waitressed before?" she asked.

I nodded and told her about my experience.

"Yes, you'll do. You're hired." She handed me my uniform—a sexy tuxedo outfit.

"You interested in dancing too?" she asked.

I looked at the skimpy clothing. This was as naked as I could get. "Oh, no, I don't think I could do that."

Her smirk said, *We'll see how long that will last.*

This was a whole new way of life for me, but I caught on fast. This was how it worked: a gentleman came in, got a table, and ordered a drink. I got him his cocktail, and if he had money, I got my favorite dancer friend to come join him. As the alcohol began to loosen him up, she made sure he ordered from me and tipped generously. It was a "you scratch my back, I'll scratch yours" relationship. But it was also a cutthroat business. I learned the unspoken rules . . . like don't mess with another girl's "regulars." Cutthroat, yet a strange sisterhood of sorts where we shared a common bond. I had a bubbly personality and had no desire to "steal" any of the dancers' men, so I became close to many of the girls. We became family. There was no judgment. It was all about survival.

The men in the club were exactly the kind of men who up to this point in my life, I thought all men were. Some of the guys who came in were innocent enough, turning twenty-one or there with their buddies for a bachelor party. But most—the big-money men, politicians, district attorneys, and law enforcement officers—were usually married. Between slipping dollar bills to the dancers and ordering another beer or whiskey, these men would try so hard to win my heart. The attention and the compliments were nice, but I knew the truth: they didn't want me—they wanted the fantasy of what they thought I was, the thrill of the forbidden, and a chance between my sheets after closing time.

I might have had low self-esteem, but even I knew I didn't want one of these guys! I only wanted their money. For a hardened, lonely single mother, it was the perfect job. I was able to work three nights a week and comfortably provide for my two children. Whenever I considered quitting, some financial burden would hit. Or maybe I got greedy. I used men. I mean, that was what you did—you made them fall in love with you and then took all you could from them. As a bonus, I thought I could use the attention of other men to make Joe jealous. My heart grew colder, and my pockets grew deeper.

Most nights I just went home, escorted to my car by the silent bouncers who were always watching, always guarding. I wasn't yet twenty-one, so I wasn't allowed to drink while I was at work—though places like this weren't so much about following the rules as they were about not getting caught breaking them. One night after closing, I was partying with some of my dancer friends and the managers of the club. They convinced me to try dancing—just once. Here tonight. A private party. Big money. So a few tequila shots later, up the stage stairs I went, dressed in five-inch heels and a skimpy G-string bikini. Loud classic rock blared from the DJ booth, and thick smoke poured out from the stage. I was scared to death!

My first tip was another double shot of tequila and a hundred-dollar bill. By the end of that Little River Band song, I already had well over a thousand dollars stuck in my G-string, and I had not even fully undressed yet. By the end of my first set, I was wasted drunk on tequila and high on money. I was no longer just a waitress.

The power that came from being on that dark, smoky stage was as intoxicating as the money. For once I was in control of the men. I could tease and seduce from center stage, where the men could look but not touch. They couldn't hurt me. In fact, I could hurt them—playing upon the anguish that came from unfulfilled sexual desire. However, to play the lively seductive woman successfully, I had to first find a way to hide the deadness inside. To do what was required of you in these places, you usually had to take something, drink something, smoke something.

Once I was hanging out with a dancer friend of mine getting high, and she really wanted some coke. I agreed to go in with her on a small amount, but I secretly prayed that the deal would not go through. Pot, that was one thing. Hard drugs were a different story. Despite my negative experiences at church, I still believed in God, and something in my conscience desperately wanted His protection.

When the deal didn't go through, I felt relieved—not because I thought drugs or sex or any part of my lifestyle was wrong, but simply because I was a scaredy-cat. I'd seen so many innocent young women come to the club, seeking a way to provide for themselves, or like me, their children. It was never long before they were sucked into sex, drugs, and alcohol, with no way out. Some became mistresses, some prostitutes. Some landed in jail. Most ended up washed up and alone. Sometimes girls would have enough, get out of the business, get a real job, and hook up with a "great guy." But often they ended up right back at the club.

I didn't want to be like that. I stayed cool. I didn't ever get into sex for money, technically. Sure, I slept with some of my customers, but I wasn't a prostitute if I didn't take money, right? I told myself I only slept with the few guys I actually liked. Again, my perception of a "good guy" was a little out of whack. I had no guilt or shame for my sexual relationships.

My relationship with God was based on a few deeply buried Bible stories. I had no thought or concern for His design for sex. I had been taught well that sex was how you fulfilled your emptiness and got men to adore you. I might have been promiscuous, but I hated sex. It made me feel dirty. It didn't fulfill the intimacy I craved. I gave my body in hopes of gaining love, which was an impossible exchange.

I convinced myself that since I was not as "bad" as the other girls, since I kept my business life and personal life separate and didn't do hard drugs, I was okay. The truth was, I didn't keep my personal life separate. I might not have allowed my children to be around the men or my coworkers, but I was deep into this lifestyle. I dressed the part, acted the part, and I was good at it. No one outside the club condemned my job or my lifestyle, at least not to my face. What could they say, really? I was making money. Had nice things. Was not on welfare. Still, I eventually decided that I wanted a more upscale club and began traveling to Dallas to work. There I would be less likely to run into my father or someone I knew.

One day I discovered I was pregnant again. I was angry that I had allowed this to happen again. *No way am I willing to have a child right now! That would mess up my life.* Pregnant dancers were not high on the most-wanted list in gentlemen's clubs. Having another child would have disrupted my life and my lifestyle. I never even told the father. I had no desire to be with him long term. There was no way I would tie myself to him for a lifetime by having his child. Plus, having a child with another man would permanently ruin my chances of reconciliation with Joe.

I called a friend, drove to Dallas, and got rid of the problem. More power, more control. It was my body, my choice. I knew full well that I was pregnant with a baby. I didn't believe it was just a blob of tissue or whatever some women are told; I simply had no plans of having this child. The ride to Dallas was silent. No condemnation, no judgment, and no trying to convince me to not have the abortion. I didn't cry this time when I was counseled. I just signed the papers and paid my fee. I did ask to see the sonogram, but they refused. *Close your eyes. Relax. It will all be over in a few minutes.* My friend agreed not to say one word about it, ever. A few days later, I was back on the stage.

Though life had hardened me, something still bothered me. *Why wouldn't they show me the sonogram?* I did some research and read stories about how an abortion doctor would sometimes do a false procedure on a woman who was not pregnant so that he would still get paid. It was absurd that would actually happen. Even more absurd that I believed it. *That must have been it. I was never really pregnant.* It was all a ruse, and I could walk away unscarred. The doctor had done a false procedure on me to get paid. The delusion was easier to face than dealing with the lie to my heart and the loss of another child. I pushed it so far down that I convinced myself it was gone.

Chapter 9

Chance Encounter
or Destiny?

A *Sam Cooke song played over* the speakers as I sat by myself on the brick patio wall in the sunny backyard of the lake house, picking at a piece of wedding cake. This reception had southern charm. Guests mingled around the backyard, celebrating the new bride and groom. The four-year-old flower girl I'd recently had to drag down the aisle raced by with the other children. Laughter from small groups echoed out every so often. Nearby, a black iron table held a three-layer cake with a blown glass swan and heart topper, and a bowl of delicious, frothy pineapple punch.

When Mandy's best friend, Penny, invited us to her wedding, I had begrudgingly agreed to attend. Our families had been friends for years, so I felt obligated. I had a date, but at the last minute, he stood me up. Just what every young woman wants—to attend a wedding single and alone.

I told myself I was okay with being alone. I didn't want another relationship! I'd already made so many mistakes that it was just easier to swear off men. Being alone was safer because I'd hurt and been hurt so much. So then why was coming to a wedding so difficult? Everything around me reminded me of the joy and love and commitment I didn't have. Deep down I still longed for that loving, romantic relationship. That was why I couldn't help but notice the bride's brother, Jay, manning the boom box on the porch. The last time I had seen him, he'd been a scrawny, freckle-faced fourteen-year-old. Like me, he'd gone a little wild through his teen years. We hadn't stayed in touch, but I'd heard he'd traveled a lot and eventually moved to Austin, Texas. He wasn't the same lanky, string bean I remembered, that was for sure! Broad shouldered and a full-grown six foot six inches, he looked sharp in his tux. I thought of the movie *Who Framed Roger Rabbit?*—the part when a homely female character ran after the detective screaming, "A maaan!" Well, that was about how I felt seeing Jay for the first time in so many years. *Whoa . . . little Jaybird is a maaan!* My heart got a little giggle in it, and I felt a little flirtatious, a little shy. Maybe not having a date wasn't such a bad thing . . .

Jay's grandma was scurrying up the porch stairs with her hands full of something, when Jay attempted to grab her for a dance. GaGa always had perfectly placed hair. She was what you would expect to see in a picture dictionary next to the words "precious pastor's wife." And that was what she was—gentle and kind and loving. Much like an elderly Mary Poppins, rosy cheeks and all! But also firm and conservative.

"Dance with me, GaGa."

She pulled back and nailed him with a glare.

"Jay, Baptists do *not* dance!" she said, playful yet stern.

"Well, this one does," he said, smiling.

Before I knew what was happening, he turned, grabbed my hand, and whisked me onto the porch-turned-dance-floor. Whirling around in his arms, I spun from a vow of singleness to knowing someday this man would be my husband, all in the matter of a breath. Somehow I knew I would be his wife. Jay and I had an instant spark. He was both a fun and funny guy—the life of the party. Oh, how he brought laughter to my lips and to my heart that day! After just one dance at a wedding that I hadn't even cared to be at, I managed to give my whole heart to Mr. Jay Garrett.

"Are you doing anything later?" he asked as he swung me around.

"Wide open," I said.

"I don't drive back to Austin until tomorrow. I'm hanging out with the guys tonight. Want to join us?"

"Sure."

That night sealed the deal, and after Jay returned to Austin, we started a long-distance relationship. I had no phone, so each evening I would walk down to the pay phone around the corner from my house, and we would talk the night away. He traveled for his job, and on July 4, he drove from Arkansas to Tyler, Texas, to take me on our official first date—a double date. We went to Cace's Seafood. I don't remember what I had, but I clearly remember him and his friend, Harley, both ordering medium-rare steaks. Steaks at a seafood place! I soaked in every detail of my time with Jay. He spent his entire paycheck on me that night. We ate, we drank, we danced, we drank, we shot fireworks, and we drank some more. In the end, we may have been pretty plastered, but we had fun!

At the time, I was still legally married to Andy. Jay refused to date another man's wife and insisted I get a divorce. While this was only natural, it meant a lot to me. *He wants me to himself!* Even though we didn't have a pure relationship, I knew Jay's views on marriage vows were incredibly sincere. His moral compass may have needed some recalibrating in some areas, but the fact that he didn't want me married to another man was attractive. It made me feel valued. Wanted. Desired. Not in the normal sleazy way I had become accustomed to, but in a protective way. No other man had ever wanted me in this way before.

As we became more serious, he also didn't want me dancing anymore. What man *would* want other men looking at what was his? Jay hated me working at the club, but he was my boyfriend, not my father. He couldn't tell me where I could and couldn't work. I remained as a waitress and dancer off and on in the club world, but mostly I tried to work "real" jobs. The only problem with real jobs was that they paid diddly-squat, so I often found myself back in the club, hustling dollar bills. I never stayed long—just long enough to make rent or pay the electric bill. Then I'd be gone again until some other need came up. I knew how to make the money, and I was good at it.

My relationship with Jay was fast paced, even though we lived hours apart. I went to Austin to visit him a time or two, but most weekends he came and stayed with me while my kids were with their dads or grandparents. We would have a wildly fun time, sharing our hopes and dreams and bodies. One night we were lying on a pallet on the floor in my living room, listening to Pink Floyd, lights out, candles glowing. He stood up and said simply, "Dance with me." I just about swooned at the pure romance of it. If there was any part of my heart not yet his, he secured it that night. I loved this man.

Only a month into our relationship, during one of our phone conversations, I told Jay I was going to marry him. "Oh yeah?" was his response.

Even though we weren't yet married, I very much felt a commitment from Jay. Unfortunately, it was a commitment I didn't honor. I might have been in love with him, convinced that I would someday be his wife, but in a moment of weakness, I got caught up in a one-night stand while he was working in Colorado. I was lonely. Maybe I felt like I was losing control because of my emotions for Jay. I was still a broken young woman searching to fill the voids in my life. I'd learned early in life that to keep from getting hurt, you sometimes had to be the one hurting others. The problem with that was, more times than not, I hurt myself alongside whomever I was trying to protect my heart from.

I'd learned how to justify my actions to avoid the guilt of them, but after I cheated on Jay, my head was filled with every terrible thing I'd done. Still, I tucked this secret inside with all my other secrets. I loved Jay so much that every ugly thing I was had to be buried deep. Jay knew about my screwed-up family, but he had no idea about any of my dark secrets—the sexual abuse, the abortions, the promiscuity, and now, the cheating.

By now, Jay and I were officially together, and I'd introduced him to my children. After he finished the job in Colorado, he came back to my apartment in Tyler instead of his place in Austin, and he never left. Ironically, he refused to admit that he was living in Tyler. When he ran into old friends and they asked if he was back, he always replied, "No, I live in Austin. I'm just staying here." For a long time he did live out of his suitcase, until, slowly but surely, his belongings found their way into their own place in my home.

Jay and I had lots of good times, and we had a pretty good relationship, considering, but honestly, I have no clue how on earth we made it. I was very independent. I had a sarcastic attitude of "I don't need you. I was fine without you, and I will be fine without you again. No one is holding you captive." To be brutally honest, I was a monster.

We continued to party a lot. I did try to protect my children, but they were unavoidably caught up in my brokenness and the life I was living. We were not abusive parents, but we were not good parents either. More importantly, we were lost spiritually. We both believed in God, even believed in Jesus Christ—that made us Christians, right?—but He had no influence or place in our day-to-day life. Having a head knowledge of God and believing He was real didn't make me a Christian any more than standing in my garage made me a car, but at that time if we were asked, we would both have professed Christianity.

About a year into our relationship, I got pregnant. Same story—again. As I looked at the home pregnancy test, my stomach churned, not with nausea but with fear, anger, and regret. I didn't want another child, because my relationships with the fathers of my two other children hadn't worked out, and I was not ready for Jay to leave me too. Yet I knew I couldn't abort another child. My heart was still too messed up from the previous abortions.

I was devastated. I cried most of the day, and by the time Jay got home from work, I was a hot mess. A hormonal, hysterical, irrational hot mess! The puzzled look on Jay's face said he didn't know what on earth was going on.

"What's wrong?" he asked.

The floodgates opened.

"I'm pregnant," I said, sobbing.

Jay paused, then started whooping and hollering. I stared at him as he jumped on the bed, dancing around and pumping his fist in the air.

"I'm going to be a dad! I'm going to be a dad!"

This is insane. He's actually excited to be a father? I was in shock.

Jay finally returned to earth enough to give me a big hug before dashing out of the room.

"I need to call the guys!"

We had tossed around plans to get married, but within weeks of finding out we were having a child, Jay decided to formally ask me to be his wife. Without a hint of romance, one Thursday afternoon about a week after my pregnancy reveal, Jay said, "Marry me."

"Okay. When?" I said.

"How about this Saturday?"

We went Friday and got our marriage license and planned for his grandfather to marry us on Saturday. We didn't realize that in the state of Texas you had to have your marriage license for three full business days before it was a legal document, so instead of changing our plans, we postdated our marriage license. We said our vows on July 27, 1998, but our legal anniversary was not until July 30, which just gave us an excuse to celebrate for three days. We'd intended to elope, but Jay's GaGa could not bear the thought of us not having at least some close family there, so she spilled the beans to his sister, and because he now had family coming, I also invited my mother. We had our best friends there as well, but that was all.

I was still an independent woman with an "I don't need you but choose you anyway" attitude, so when Jay's grandfather had me repeat after him that little line of "to honor and obey," I did what I thought all strong, independent women would do . . . I giggled. I actually thought he was joking. Turns out he wasn't! Well, I did repeat those words, not knowing how I would grow to cherish them and the family I'd just become part of.

None of our family thought we should be together or that we would stay together. I found out later that his family, especially his grandparents, didn't want us together. I'd believed that they wanted us married because they didn't approve of us living together, but turned out they would have preferred we weren't together at all. Not that I could argue with their reasoning. I was trash, and the Garretts were not. Had I been in their shoes, I would never in a bazillion years want my grandson to marry a girl like I was. Yet the Garretts never let on that they disliked me. They showed me love and accepted my children.

GaGa took Ashlei and Austin, set them on her lap, and told them that now that Jay and I were married, she would be their GaGa! I never forgot the sound of her words. She wanted us. Jay wanted us. Maybe family *could* be different than what I'd known.

Chapter 10

Fraud and Forgiveness

"Hello, this is the Smith County Court. Is this Billy Jo White?"

I propped the phone against my shoulder. I hadn't heard my maiden name in a while. "Yes, this is she."

"Ms. White, we're calling to inform you that you need to appear in court tomorrow regarding the theft by check that was never resolved."

This again? I sighed. I knew exactly what this was about; I just hadn't expected it to still be following me. Years earlier I had been pulled over on my way to meet a date. It was my first time being pulled over, and I had cried, not sure what to do. The police officer was kind, but after running my name, he came back with bad news.

"Ma'am, I'm sorry. I'm going to have to place you under arrest and take you in."

What?!

I had no clue what was going on, only that he'd said I had a warrant for a "theft by check." When I got to court, all the legal folks tried to get me to plead guilty. I was young, they said, and I would just get a slap on the wrist. But I didn't know what the check was for or even how much. In fact, I didn't even know what "theft by check" meant. I was no thief! I asked the district attorney if I could at least see the check, and when she handed it to me, I recognized the distinctive handwriting—my mother's.

When I saw my check signed with my name in her handwriting, the hatred bubbled up in my chest. All those Christmas gifts she'd lavished on my Ashlei a few years earlier? She'd stolen a check from my wallet, gone to Walmart, and written a hot check in my name. What kind of monster stole from her own daughter? Now I'd been arrested because of it.

My mother bailed me out, ironically, and a week later I went to court. For that whole week, my mother knew why I had been arrested and what I was facing, but she played ignorant and did nothing. Why didn't she intervene? You would think that since this was her fault, she would have gone to the authorities and owned up to the crime to protect me. But then, protecting me was never her parenting style.

I didn't plead guilty as I was being pressured to do, but I also didn't turn my mother in. I had to go through lots of handwriting tests and sign affidavits, but I did not—would not—take the blame. Since that time, I'd believed this had all been dropped; I thought my mother had gotten away with yet another crime. But no. The court was after me again.

My relationship with my mother had not improved, but one thing had changed—she'd been diagnosed with cancer. I didn't care. I refused to pay for her crime. This didn't go over well with the rest of my mother's family. Didn't I know she was dying? Didn't I care? How could I expect her to make this right?

I didn't care if she was dying. This was her fault, her problem, and I was not going to jail for this woman. I was finally happily married and trying to have a decent, normal life. I called her up.

"Mom, you need to confess, or I'm going to tell the courts that you're the one who wrote that hot check."

Fraud and Forgiveness

One way or the other, the truth was finally coming out. She did write a letter to the court, and eventually I was completely released from all charges. Because of her health, she did not have to do any jail time. I might have been cleared of the charges, but my heart hadn't been cleared of the resentment I felt toward my mother.

Several months later, Jay and I took the kids out to eat and ran into her at the restaurant. I hadn't seen or spoken to her since the court case. The cancer had progressed, and she was now in a wheelchair, hooked to a portable IV. She barely resembled the woman I knew as my mother, but I felt no sadness or compassion for her.

"Nanny!" Ashlei and Austin ran up to her, and her face lit up. They saw her only occasionally, so they were excited.

But I wasn't. I was still so full of anger that I shooed my kids away and shunned her, refusing to acknowledge her. I knew how much she loved being a grandmother, because of the way she loved Mandy's daughters, so I knew this would hurt her. I wanted her to feel unwanted the same way she'd made me feel unwanted. In my heart I felt like she deserved to rot. I wanted her to die. Before we left, I saw the look of pure brokenness on my mother's face. She sat at her table crying instead of eating, but I refused to let myself feel anything but revulsion. The raw emptiness I felt toward her reflected a blackness in my heart, weighed down by years of emotional trauma.

That encounter at the restaurant was the last contact I had with her until the week before she died. I was at home one afternoon when Mandy called, begging me to go see our mother. I didn't want to see her, but my sister convinced me that I needed to go. "Do you want to live with this the rest of your life? Do you want to carry the guilt and burden of unforgiveness?" I went with the intention to simply say goodbye and leave. But when I walked into that mobile home that afternoon, I was not prepared for the flood of emotions that assaulted me.

A hospice nurse met me at the door.

"She's awake right now."

I gave a curt nod toward David, my mother's husband, and slipped into the bedroom. It looked ordinary—a dresser against the wall with a television stand, piles of clutter, a door to the closet. But the night-stand overflowed with bottles of medication, a veritable pharmacy. The withered, defeated, shell of a woman who lay in the bed was barely recognizable as my mother.

I lost it. Years of pure unrestrained hurt, anger, and fear poured out in gushing sobs. I sank into a chair near her bedside with the realization of how heavy this burden of hatred was. What did it accomplish? Suddenly, nothing mattered anymore.

My mother couldn't speak, but through the blur of my tears, I could tell she recognized me. I saw relief on her face, as if she knew she would never see me again and was relieved that I'd made it. I looked at her and then patted my belly. I was five months pregnant now and hadn't told her yet.

"Mom, you're going to have another granddaughter."

Her eyes widened, and she weakly reached her arm out to touch my stomach. I placed her hand on my tummy, and the baby somer-saulted the moment she touched me, as if to introduce herself to the nanny she would never meet. There were no more words, just tears in both our eyes. She mouthed, I love you, and I wept.

I love you too, Mom.

Nothing could erase the scars I still carried from the way she hadn't protected me from sexual abuse, and I still hurt, but deep down I loved her. I thought back on life with my mother. I couldn't excuse the hor-rible things she'd done, but for the first time I began to see the twisted love in her motivations. The check she stole? She couldn't handle the thought of her grandchild spending a Christmas without any presents from her. When she went to jail for stealing cigarettes? They were for my sister, not for her. She didn't even smoke. When she stole identities and some new name showed up on our mail? It was so she could get the utilities turned back on. In her mind she must have believed she was doing the best she could to provide for us girls.

Even when I hated my mother, I knew I could call her; she would not turn me away. I turned her away many times, but she always took me in. After my first abortion, I had called my mom many times and just cried. I am sure she knew I had killed her grandchild, but she didn't address it. She just listened to me cry until I had no tears left. It was little things like this that came to mind as I sat at her deathbed.

She was my mom, and she did love me, and I was about to lose her. The fact that my baby daughter would never know her grandmother . . . it was a hard pill to swallow. I'd kept Ashlei and Austin from her because of my hatred. But this new daughter would be kept from her because she was dying. That was different. Worse.

Mandy had been right. I needed closure and forgiveness as much as my mother did. But for all my superficial professions of faith, I really didn't understand anything about forgiveness. In that moment at her bedside, I didn't acknowledge that I needed to forgive her, and I don't think I even realized that I *had* forgiven her. It just sort of happened. I felt a peace that made no sense and a love that I couldn't explain. Perhaps what I recognized the most was the absence of hate.

Before I walked in and saw her, I had very much believed in a fire-filled place called hell and fully felt my mom belonged there. After seeing her, I just wanted her *not* to die so I could somehow steal back wasted time that I'd lost because of my own choices. I believed in heaven too, but we didn't talk about spiritual things, other than the cliché of a "better place." I had no clue how a person got to heaven or hell. Mom had gone back to church after I married Jay, but I had strayed further, coming to a place of contempt for church and religion. I had few examples of true believers in my life. The ones that I did know, I just considered good people. Nice people were Christians, and mean people were not. No Jesus needed. No faith required.

I spent the next week caring for my mother. It was an awful week of both death and healing, during which I came to see that in her own way, my mother was honestly remorseful for the life she had led us through. Much as I hadn't wanted to admit it, I had noticed that she was different when she took responsibility for the check she'd stolen from me. She could have refused to own up to it, but she confessed. She was different when I shunned her at the restaurant. The hurt in her eyes reflected a broken heart, no hint of pride or manipulation. Perhaps she had truly repented and found grace and forgiveness from Someone else when she hadn't received it from me.

I had craved that remorse from her my whole life. Finally in the end, I had a taste of it. I served her in the most intimate ways during her last days, showing her compassion that only a forgiving heart could express. My mother died knowing that I had finally found it in my heart to forgive her. When death released her, so did I.

Chapter 11

On the Rocks

With my mother gone and no real relationship with my father, I no longer had any ties to East Texas. After I gave birth to our daughter, Alexandria—named after my mother to honor the good she possessed—Jay decided to move our family to Austin so he could go into business with a friend. I was happy to follow him anywhere, but I also had an ulterior motive. The real reason I was so willing to run off to Austin was because I knew that I could inflict pain on Joe by moving away with our son. As much as he hadn't initially wanted to be a father, he actually did love Austin, so I knew our moving away would break his heart.

I might have reconciled with my mother, but I was still bitter toward Joe. I still wanted him to taste the hurt he had inflicted on me— first by not wanting our first child and not stopping me from taking his innocent little life, and then by sleeping with other women while I was expecting. He had never shown an ounce of remorse for any of it. Of course, I didn't consider our son's heart in this matter. I was more concerned with vengeance than I was about the precious lives I was damaging.

I moved to Austin ahead of Jay to get a job and find us a place to live. I quickly found an apartment and, after bouncing around a few jobs, became a manager at Whataburger, but the apartment wouldn't be ready for about a month, so I stayed with the guys—Jay's friends. I grew to love these guys like true brothers.

They loved us, and we were close, but once Jay and the kids moved and we became a family of five in their bachelor pad, it wasn't the easiest arrangement for any of us. But it was only for a month—you can endure anything for a month, right? The problem was, by the time that month was over, the apartment manager had made a mistake and given our apartment to someone else. What a nightmare!

We ended up living in a hotel room for months. Paying weekly hotel rates made it impossible to save up enough to move out. I had a hot plate and a microwave to cook meals. It was not fun, but it was a place to live, and ultimately we survived. During that time, I started visiting a church in order to ask for assistance. I began working in the nursery for a little extra money. This felt better than getting a handout. It made me less like my mom. I became close to some of the members, and they helped us get out of the hotel. But even after we moved into a house, we continued to struggle.

Jay's business partner got strung out on drugs, and things were not going well at all. We had a nice Jeep that we could no longer afford, and eventually it was repossessed. Less than a week after we lost it, the motor in my car blew. I spent the next few months traveling by bus to buy groceries with an infant, to take Ashlei to school, to go to the laundromat. There were days at a time when I had nothing to feed my kids but a little rice or ramen noodles.

My connections at church were complicated too. I was so lost that the "perfect" pastor and his "perfect" wife struggled to relate to me. They probably spoke the truth in love, but I felt judged and hurt by their words. I was too broken for their church and ultimately felt unwelcome. I never went back.

This was not how I had seen it in my mind when we decided to move to Austin. I cried every day that year.

My son, Austin, went back to Tyler to stay with Joe every other weekend, and he was happier there. They had big TVs, computers, video games, food—you know, all the things kids like to have. After months of fighting, I finally allowed Austin to move in with his dad. It broke my heart to give him up. When Joe sent me papers to sign to enroll Austin in school, I didn't question him. We had joint custody, but as it turned out, the papers I signed gave him primary conservator rights. Joe promised that this was temporary, and as soon as Jay and I were back on our feet, he would let Austin come back home. He lied.

I felt like I'd lost my son, and that added to the misery I felt living in Austin. I blamed Jay for moving us to this awful town, which didn't help, because Jay was miserable too. He had expected our family life there to be as fun as the weekend trips we used to take, but *living* here was no vacation. He had friends, but they had no desire to hang out with a boring family with small children. Jay started drinking more, and when I found out that he had tried cocaine, that was the last bit of ammunition I needed. I was done with Austin, Texas.

A friend in Huntsville—a few hours away—offered me a place to stay. It took only a few phone calls to transfer my job.

"I'm leaving," I told Jay. "You can come with me or not, but I'm outta here."

Thankfully, Jay chose to leave with me, so we packed up and left Austin—forever, as far as I was concerned. I had no desire to ever go back there again.

I took a significant pay cut when I transferred my job because the pay scale was lower and because I was demoted from manager to assistant manager. I didn't care! Anything was better than life in Austin. Jay got a job as a maintenance man, and we were able to move into a nice little duplex. I enjoyed life in Huntsville, but Jay did not. He was slipping into full-blown alcoholism. Thinking back, he was most likely an alcoholic long before we married. Unlike Tyler, Huntsville was a "wet" town. So just as I was able to pull up to any store or gas station for a diet Dr Pepper, Jay was able to pull up and grab a beer. Or ten. And he did this often, using the alcohol to numb his pain.

One night he was out drinking with some friends, and I was supposed to pick them up after the bar closed. I got sick that night—to the point of throwing up—and was late to get him. I drove around looking for him and eventually found him and his friends walking home. I wasn't happy about hunting for my drunk-as-always husband while I felt unwell. He wasn't happy about being stranded by his wife. Put us together, and we were tinder and kindling, ready for an explosive fight.

"I'm going to bed," I said when we got home. Maybe I could ignore him until he was sober. *Yeah, right.* Ignoring a drunk was impossible. Jay followed me into the bedroom.

"What the hell were you doing? Why didn't you pick us up?" he slurred as I lay down on the bed.

"I was puking my guts up! Sorry I didn't stop in time to pick your drunk ass up from the freaking club." I turned and pulled the covers over me. "Please leave me alone. I'm done with this."

Jay came around to face me, murder in his eyes.

"I'll kill you before you take my daughter away from me."

"What the hell are you talking about, Jay?"

Something in him snapped. Jay was irritating when he was drunk, for sure, but he was never violent. But now he reached down and put his hands on my throat.

"Don't you dare threaten to take our daughter away from me. I could kill you right now, and no one would ever know."

I gasped. This wasn't my husband. I mean, it was him, but it wasn't. Something else had taken him over. It terrified me.

Within seconds Jay released me, stepped back, and looked down at his hands, an expression of horror on his face. It was as if he snapped back into himself and was instantly sober and appalled at his actions.

"Billy Jo, I'm so sorry. I didn't mean that. I don't know what came over me."

I'd never even considered taking Alex away from him, but his threat had me reconsidering. He kept apologizing and begging me to forgive him.

"It's fine," I said. But it wasn't. Already my mind was making plans to escape, if I could survive this night. I would not spend my life in fear.

"I promise I won't ever have another drink," he assured me. "Please don't leave me."

I didn't believe that was possible, but I lied and said I would stay.

A week or so later, Ashlei's grandmother, Jackie, came down for a visit, and I had every intention of going back home with her to Tyler. She, of course, knew nothing about our marital struggles or my plan. Being her ever-helpful self, she insisted Jay and I go on a date.

"I'll watch the kids," she said, brushing aside my excuses. "What are MawMaws for?"

That date saved our marriage. I didn't know what exactly made me stay. I couldn't imagine that he would give up drinking. It was part of who he was. He always had a drink in hand. But Jay begged for the chance to prove that he loved us more than alcohol. We talked, we cried, and I relented.

Jay made good on his promise. The next year was kind of weird, with Jay not drinking. It was like he didn't know how to function anymore. He'd always been drinking, and now, here he was, completely sober. To be honest, he was boring! I didn't want him to ever drink again—in fact, I was serious that if he ever did, I would leave—but I did miss parts of the old him. Not the drunk him . . . just him. He wasn't the same guy I'd fallen in love with.

I took advantage of this new Jay to drink more myself. Because I had spent so many nights sober, babysitting my drunk husband, I thought it was my turn to enjoy life a little. I pushed the limits and drank just to test him. Those first few months, I was trying to see how strong he was. Could he really *not* drink? Thankfully, my wild side was short lived. Eventually I began to believe that something, or Someone, had removed Jay's desire for alcohol.

Jay did his best to be a good husband, but he had no clue how to lead our family. Jay's parents had divorced when he was young, and he'd never seen what a healthy marriage looked like. He did have the example of godly grandparents, but no daily in-home examples of how to be a good husband or what to even hope for in a good wife.

And I was not a good wife. I had never witnessed a healthy marriage in action either. I never gave him the right to lead our family or to be the main provider. Instead, I tried to be a good mother. I still very much had the attitude that these were my kids, and I would take care of them.

I spent most weekends driving to Tyler to visit my son. Nearly immediately after Austin moved home to live with his dad, he had regretted his choice and wanted to come back home. My heart broke every time I tried to explain to my crying little boy that he couldn't come to live with me. Jay and I were stable now, able to buy groceries and pay our bills, and I'd asked Joe over and over to let Austin move back in with me, but to no avail. Finally, one day I got an answer.

"I'll let Austin live with you again as soon as you move back to Tyler."

Immediately I began making plans to relocate back to East Texas. If this was what it took to be reunited with my son, there was no question in my mind about my course of action. A good wife probably would have consulted her husband, but I'm ashamed to admit that I would have moved with just my daughters had Jay resisted. I prioritized motherhood over marriage.

Fortunately, Jay was supportive, and we made plans to rent a small mobile home from a friend in Bullard, about half an hour from Tyler. We would rent a home, move in, get my son back, and live happily ever after, right? Not quite . . . Nothing in my life was ever as simple as it should be.

Chapter 12

Into the Fire

What is that terrible smell?

I'd just unlocked the door to our new home, only to be greeted by a wave of putrid air. Stepping over the threshold, I looked around. The previous tenants had left weeks ago but had left their dogs—a mama with a new litter of pups. Feces littered the carpet alongside bits of kibble from a bag that had been dumped out for them. I choked and pressed my nose into my elbow as I stepped carefully across the room into the kitchen. Pulling open a drawer revealed a layer of mouse droppings. Jay and the moving truck were due in a few days, but this wasn't livable. What a mess!

I had no time for a pity party. Instead, I loaded up on bleach and cleaner and trash bags, pulled on my gloves, and got busy. I had to pull up all the carpet where the dogs had been and empty the vacuum canister between each drawer of mouse droppings. Disgusting! I worked for three days around the clock, only stopping for gag breaks and for the occasional breath of fresh air required for survival. By the time Jay pulled up with the kids and our belongings, I'd managed to at least make the house fit for human habitation. It wasn't large but had three bedrooms, two baths, and a decent living room and kitchen area. We could make it comfortable and homey. Most importantly, it was only a short distance from my son.

But after we'd finished arranging the furniture and putting the last dish away and hanging the photo frames on the wall, Joe didn't keep his promise to let Austin live with me again. I am not sure why I had ever thought he would. I consoled myself by focusing on the fact that I was closer to visit, so in the end it was still better.

Only a few months after moving into our new house, I had a terrible nightmare. Stifling blackness. Nothingness. Vulnerable, alone, empty. I couldn't breathe, couldn't move, paralyzed with fear, and trapped in the bed by an immovable force. It was as if I was looking in at something that was coming.

Death.

I awoke in sheer panic, covered in sweat. Jay stirred next to me as I gulped in deep breaths of air to calm myself down.

It was a dream. Just a dream.

But the dream lingered into the next morning, and I couldn't shake the feeling that it was more than an unsettling nightmare. It felt like a premonition of my impending death; a warning. A warning I couldn't shake. *Am I going to die?*

I stuffed the thought aside and headed out on a shopping trip with Ashlei. By noon I'd managed to distract myself from the dream—that is, until we pulled into a Burger King to meet Jay, and *wham!* A crunch of metal jolted my head and my heart. A teenage girl had whipped around in a U-turn and hit us. I looked over at Ashlei.

"You okay?"

She nodded, eyes wide. I clutched the steering wheel with trembling hands, gathering my wits. *I'm okay. I'm alive.*

That night, still messed up by the dream of dying and the shock of the day, I didn't want to go to bed. After putting the kids down, I found a book to read and settled into the tub for a soak. The warm water soothed my tense muscles, and the book distracted my mind for a little while. Finally, when I could barely keep my eyes open, I got ready for bed. Jay was already asleep, and with him, three-year-old Alex. I scooped her up gently so as not to wake her, but instead of taking her to her own bed, I laid her on the couch, which was closer. I returned to my own bed, pure exhaustion taking over as I slipped under the covers.

Shoot, I left the door open.

We normally closed our bedroom door at night, but I was too tired to get back up.

Oh well. It can stay open tonight.

I nestled into the pillow and immediately fell asleep.

I'm not sure why or how I woke up, but something peaceful nudged me awake. I squinted at the neon numbers on the clock. I had been asleep only about half an hour. I forced my eyes open, and they stung. *Smoke.* Even in the darkness, I could see a cloud of black smoke obscuring our ceiling. *Is this another nightmare? Am I going to die?*

I reached over and shook Jay awake. He jumped up and pulled on his robe.

"Billy Jo, the house is on fire!"

I froze. This was no dream.

Jay was already to the doorway.

"Billy Jo, get Alex!" he barked, then disappeared down the hallway.

Alex! I leaped from the bed and grabbed my daughter off the couch, where she was still peacefully asleep. Jay appeared with Ashlei and shoved us out the front door. Ten-foot tongues of flame spewed out the door behind us and began to lick up the walls of our house. We stumbled out into the darkness. I didn't know fire could be this loud. It roared and hissed and cracked.

Once we were a safe distance away, Jay turned back.

"I'm going to see if I can grab some clothes or save any part of the house."

"Jay, no!"

But he was already running back. I saw him at the front door. Had he gone inside? I was a wreck. Within a few minutes, a huge boom exploded all the windows in the house. *Was Jay trapped inside? Was he hurt?*

Through the flames, I heard him scream, "Call for help!"

I pulled Alex and Ashlei to the edge of the road.

"Stay here and don't move until I get back."

Their faces mirrored the panic they must have seen in mine. I stumbled across a field to the neighbor's house. We had never spoken, but here I was in the wee hours of the night banging on their door, crying for help.

"Help, my house . . . we were asleep . . . the fire . . . can I use your phone?" I stuttered to the man who opened the door. He was already dressed.

"I've already called for help. The fire department is on the way."

We ran together back toward the burning building, and I grabbed Ashlei and Alex on the way.

When we arrived, I grabbed my neighbor's arm. "Please, my husband is in there," I said, sobbing. He disappeared into the smoke.

Time stood still. The horrid fear from my dream had become a reality. But now it was Jay's life I feared for, instead of my own. Alex cried into my shoulder, and Ashlei clung to me.

"Where's Dad?" she asked.

"It's going to be okay," I said. *It has to be okay.*

What seemed like a lifetime later, the fire department blasted into the yard, sirens wailing. When the flames subsided, I saw Jay and our neighbor come around the side of the house. They had been in the back, fighting the fire with a broken water hose. I hugged him tighter than I ever had. He was unscathed, other than a few burns and cuts on his bare feet from when the windows exploded. We were all free from harm.

Once the fire was extinguished, I wanted to go inside the house to see if we could salvage anything. All I had on my mind was cleaning up the mess so we could get moved back in. I'd done it once; I could do it again. Right?

Into the Fire

At first the firefighters wouldn't allow me to go in. Only about forty-five minutes had passed since that first smell of smoke.

"Mrs. Garrett, it's really not a good idea for you to go inside."

But I went in against their advice, and the devastating reality began to sink in. It looked worse than when I'd first arrived to filth and feces. The fire had blazed an irregular trail through the rooms. Some items were only inches away from each other, yet one was destroyed beyond recognition and the other untouched. Our family game cupboard had burned, but a bag of marshmallows one cabinet over had not even melted. The plush cream-colored sofa didn't burn at all, but the blanket lying on it that Alex had been wrapped in was scorched. The wolf painting by Jay's dad? Ruined. The freezer full of food? Melted shut and covered in black soot. What the fire did not destroy, the smoke and water damage did.

At least we still have some clothes, I thought, until after washing and rewashing, I still couldn't get out the smell of smoke. We literally had nothing but the clothes on our backs.

We didn't have insurance, but the American Red Cross gave us vouchers for new clothes at Target, provided a new refrigerator, and helped us with the first month's rent at our new place. Friends and strangers we'd never even met gave us dishes, bedding, and money. The local news station wanted to air a story to help us, but when I discovered their agenda was to make us look like the poor family who'd lost everything and needed handouts, I refused to do the interview. We *were* that, but the last thing I wanted was charity. Didn't matter if it was from a church or not. Besides, the video cameras might capture the destruction that so perfectly expressed my heart, my life. I would rather go without.

As the shock of the fire wore off, I began to reflect on the events of that night. There were small details that had seemed unimportant on the surface—coincidental even—yet they had made the difference between life and death. If I'd laid Alex in her bed instead of on the couch, she would have been dead before we even knew the house was on fire.

My son and nephew had planned to spend the night with us, but plans had changed at the last minute. Had they been there, they would have been asleep on the top bunk—the bunk that the next day was solid black. Had I gotten up to close our bedroom door instead of leaving it open, our entire house could have been gone before a hint of smoke reached us, since it was an older home and the door had no vents.

Our home and all we owned may have been a complete loss, but we were safe. My premonition of death had made its pass, but I had prevailed . . . or had been protected. I didn't acknowledge God's providence at the time, but He surely was looking out for me and my family.

Chapter 13

The Sweet Life

"Here it is," Debbie said, pushing open the front door to the house.

I stepped into the entryway and took in the clean, empty room. When Jay and I had first decided to move back to East Texas, we had wanted to rent this house. Debbie, the owner, was a friend of ours, but she and her mother were using it to store merchandise for their business at the time, and it hadn't been available. While their business was still thriving, the house was now vacant—great timing considering we'd lost our house to the fire only a week ago.

"It's beautiful," I said, following Debbie into the living room. With four bedrooms, a gated community, and a lake nearby, this was nicer than most places I'd lived.

"I'll have to introduce you to our neighbor, Nikki," Debbie said. "I know you haven't been happy at your job, and she needs another waitress to work at the teahouse in Bullard that she owns."

Once again, I'd been working at the club, much as Jay hated it. I was growing to hate it too. Debbie knew that I had waited tables forever, but she didn't know where.

"Yeah, I'm interested. Will you give her my number?"

We moved in that weekend. Little did I know, the fire had transplanted me to the "Christian Triangle." Our new house sat on the corner of an intersection. Debbie lived across the road, Nikki and her plant nursery were diagonal across the intersection, and a block down the road was a church.

We were still settling in when Nikki called. After about five minutes of conversation, she said, "Can you start Tuesday?"

She hasn't even met me! I don't even know where this teahouse is.

"Yes," I said.

When I arrived for work the next week, I discovered the teahouse was also a garden nursery. Outside, potted plants hung from every perch, and flowers of every kind and color carpeted the ground. A path led to a gazebo with white lattice, surrounded by benches and stonework and water features. After the loud, smoky environment of the club, this place was a paradise.

A short, spunky woman with close-cropped hair met me at the door.

"Hi, I'm Nikki. Come on in."

She led me through a heavily wallpapered room, past long tables draped with linen tablecloths and adorned with vases of flowers, and laid out with place settings.

As Nikki showed me the ropes over the next few days, it didn't take me long to discover that every lady I worked with was a lover of Jesus Christ. And most of the customers too. If the Christian music playing in the dining room wasn't a giveaway, the fact that most guests prayed before their meals was. Every day after we closed, the staff sat down to eat, and someone would always bless the food. I had usually demolished half of my croissant sandwich before I realized I was the only one eating. No one ever scolded me about it. I'd seen people pray, but not like this. This was real.

Nikki was a good boss. She wasn't perfect, but she was authentic. She would get mad at her husband but then forgive him; she got annoyed with customers but then got over it; she got frustrated with her family and adult children but continued to love them.

This was all so foreign to me. People didn't love so freely in my world. Kindness had always cost me something. But not here—not with Nikki. She just loved me because she loved Jesus. And she was funny! She always had something witty to say and could pop off a one-liner comeback in about any circumstance. Nikki was the first Christian I met who was flat-out silly. I didn't know Christians were allowed to be so lighthearted. But there she was, always making us laugh till we cried. She never asked me about my past. My past didn't matter, because she loved who I was.

Though my mask was in place, it must have been obvious to them that I was lost. Sure, I knew who Jesus was. I'd always believed in God and that Jesus was God's Son and that He died on the cross. I had head knowledge of all the right stuff. But I didn't *believe* in Him, and I surely didn't trust Him for anything, especially not for salvation.

"Would you like to come to church with me?" one of my coworkers asked after I'd been working there a few months. "You'll know some people because most of the others here go to the same church."

Her church happened to be the one across the corner from my house.

I carefully placed the fine china teacups onto a tray.

"Sure, I'd love to visit your church," I lied. I had no intention of going to church. Memories of being called a whore by that self-righteous pastor when I was fifteen came to mind. Judgmental words from perfect people echoed in my mind. *You'll be unwanted, unwelcome, as always.* I was not about to try again.

So I didn't show up to church that Sunday, and then I dreaded going back to work the following Tuesday. I was sure they would hate me and judge me for not showing up as I had promised. I even considered quitting to avoid facing my coworkers, except that I desperately needed this job—not to mention, I loved it. On Tuesday morning, I dragged myself into work, avoiding eye contact with the other women. But no one mentioned my lie. They were the same kind people they always were. A few days later, one of the ladies simply said, "We missed you Sunday." And that was all. No questions or demands for excuses. Just love. I didn't know what to think.

The more I was around these ladies, the more I began to hunger for more. More of what, I wasn't sure. Maybe more of Jesus? In my experience, kindness had never been free. Nothing was ever free. For a long time, I waited for the catch—what did they want from me? What was all this sweetness going to cost me? Turns out it didn't cost me (or them) anything! Jesus had somehow changed these women into people who loved with no strings attached. I could hardly make sense of such a foreign concept.

It wasn't too long before someone invited me to another church function—an informal fish dinner and a train ride for the kids. *That sounds fun. Maybe I'll give this a try.*

The weirdest thing happened when I showed up. I met more real Christians! Just normal, everyday people who were nice and fun and loved Jesus. I was drawn to people like this. I was starving for redemption, though I had no clue what that was or how to get it. All I knew was these people had something I wanted.

I came back on Sunday. And the Sunday after that. After several months of faithful attendance, Nikki approached me one day at work.

"Have you considered joining our church?"

"I'm ready to join. How do I do that?"

"It's simple. You know how the pastor gives altar calls during the service, when people can come forward for prayer or to be saved? Just go forward and tell him you want to join. You can join by transferring a letter of membership from another church or by making a statement of faith."

I'm already a Christian, I thought, *so that should be easy.*

That next Sunday, I made my way down the aisle as the music played at the end of the service.

"I want to join the church," I said.

The Sweet Life

"Do you need to be baptized?" the pastor asked me.

Umm, duh—yes. I said I want to join the church. I'd been baptized at every church we'd joined when I was a child, so I thought each time you joined a church you had to be baptized.

"Yes," I said.

I had no clue that that answer would be what ended up saving my life. Because I said I needed to be baptized, he assumed that I needed to be saved. He was right, though I didn't know it. I thought it was just a formality. He had me repeat a simple prayer. I had no memory of ever saying a prayer like this. I confessed I was a sinner, said I believed Jesus died on the cross for my sins and rose from the dead, and promised to make Him Lord of my life. For the first time in my life, I was asking Jesus to be real in me and to do exactly what I needed Him to do—to save me.

When I walked out of the church afterward, my friends from the teahouse seemed especially excited at this next step. Nikki hugged me with tears in her eyes. *What was the big deal?* I had no clue I'd just given my heart to Jesus. I only thought I'd joined the church.

I was baptized soon after, and it was then I realized something strange had happened to me. I was so spiritually illiterate that I didn't fully understand that baptism was a symbolic act of obedience, following Jesus in His death, burial, and resurrection, but I did experience how life changing it was. As I was buried under that fresh, clean water, I honestly felt every disgusting, nasty, filthy thing throughout my life being washed away. As the pastor pulled me up out of that baptismal water, for the first time in my life, I felt clean. I mean really clean. The sexual abuse—washed. The promiscuity and abortions—washed. The dancing at the club—washed. I was a brand-new person.

The moment I realized I was different happened one Sunday after church. I ran to the grocery store down the road to pick up a few things for our lunch, and as I often did, I also purchased a package of my favorite candy—peanut M&Ms. My stomach was already rumbling, and this snack would hold me over.

97

"Could you pull out the bag of M&Ms?" I asked the sweet buggy boy who was loading the groceries into my trunk. He dug through the bags. Because this was a small-town grocery store, he knew me by name.

"Mrs. Garrett, I can't find them. Here, I'll run inside and grab you another package."

He returned within a few minutes, bag in hand.

"Thank you," I said. Crisis averted, I drove home munching on my after-church chocolate.

But when I got home and unloaded the grocery bags into the cupboards, I faced a new crisis. There, plain as could be, was the original bag of M&Ms. The old me would have been ecstatic to have scored a free bag of the treasured treats, but the new me was horrified that I'd stolen a sixty-six-cent bag of candy. I immediately called the store to explain what happened, apologize, and promise to return the stolen goods.

I truly intended to do just that, but unfortunately, even as a newly transformed child of the Most High, I could not resist a bag of M&Ms, and demolished them before I made it back to the store. I did, however, go back to bare my sinner's heart and pay for the already-eaten stolen candy. The cashier must have thought I was insane.

Maybe I was crazy, but I didn't care. This first taste of unconditional love, of authentic Christian community, was as addicting as any chocolate candy, and it was already changing me. All my life I'd struggled with feeling unwanted and unloved, and that only made this new relationship with Love that much sweeter.

Chapter 14

Food and Friends

The smell of hamburger patties on the grill wafted into the church kitchen where I stood slicing tomatoes. Across the counter was a petite woman with brown hair and an air of peacefulness. I'd seen her around church, and her husband, Tom, taught the adult Sunday school class.

"You teach the children's Sunday school class, right?" I asked.

"Yes. I'm Marilyn," she responded, smiling.

I'd peeked into the class a few times. Partly to get a glimpse of her energetic teaching, and partly to see the amazement on Austin's and Alex's faces as they watched Ms. Marilyn bring these Bible stories alive using her bright flannelgraph story board. Ashlei was in the youth department, but the younger two can still retell the stories they learned while in Marilyn's Sunday school class. Marilyn seemed to have a quiet, reserved personality, but with the kids, she was animated and lively. She had this special way of teaching deep spiritual truths and dynamic Bible stories with calmness and crazy passion all at the same time.

Marilyn nodded toward my tomatoes. "So how did you come to

start cooking Wednesday night meals?"

I carefully arranged the slices on a plate and pulled another tomato from the bag.

"I've worked in food service off and on since I was fifteen, but more importantly, I love to cook, and I saw a need."

At first, I hadn't considered cooking a gift or a talent, but I'd begun to recognize that I had the spiritual gift of service. I'd started Wednesday night dinners mostly as a way to attract students who might not come to church without the draw of free food. At first it had been just me. Slowly, others had joined in the ministry. Marilyn had started showing up, naturally and unobtrusively inserting herself into my life.

Marilyn and I ended up working together every week preparing food. I thought I'd signed up to serve in ministry, but it turned out I'd signed up to be mentored. Marilyn had a kind, gentle temperament—nothing like mine—and seemed genuinely interested in my life. Not that I would tell her anything about the old me. As we stood at that counter, mixing cookie dough or chopping vegetables or marinating chicken, she began to pour into me and teach me. I was so hungry to learn spiritual truths, and she was who the Lord chose to speak into my life.

Marilyn taught me biblical principles for being a mother and wife. She taught me the gift of biblical submission and the importance of purity within marriage. She also taught me the beauty and importance of God's special gift of intimacy between a husband and a wife. This was fantastic yet also disturbing, because the more I learned about the Lord and how His rules were gifts intended to protect us, not to limit or harm us, the more I realized how dirty and rotten I had been before I knew Him. I was like a dry, withered-up sponge, and each drop of spiritual truth she gifted to me was refreshing nourishment to my soul.

Out of all the things Marilyn taught me, teaching me how to pray was her biggest gift. She prayed for *everything*. Stubbed your toe? Let's pray. Want good weather for an event? Let's pray. What to make for dinner? Let's pray. Whenever a small need came up in conversation,

Marilyn would literally stop everything to grab my hands and pray. At first this was crazy weird to me. I was bashful and not used to this. I was also uncomfortable talking to God, especially about simple things. Well—honestly, about all things. I was just beginning to learn who God truly was, and to see and hear her stop so often to bring *all the things* she or we faced to such a Holy God—it was uncomfortable yet intriguing. Could God really care what I cooked for dinner? Did He really care that I would learn to serve my family and honor my husband? Not in a humiliating, I-am-beneath-them way, but in a humble, I-want-to-be-like-Jesus way.

With Marilyn's help, I began to learn that my heavenly Father cared about all the details of my life, all the struggles I faced, and all the memories of my past that still held me captive.

The first time I ever prayed out loud was with Marilyn. The mere thought of praying out loud with a friend scared me to death—like throw-up-and-pass-out kind of scared. Usually, we'd sit holding hands, and she would pray. When she finished, I'd quickly cap her prayer with an "Amen," say goodbye, change the subject, or hop up to start cooking again—whatever I needed to do to get out of doing "my turn." Most of the time, I was so nervous that I couldn't even concentrate on her prayers! I knew the intent was for us to both pray, but I never could. Nothing would come out.

Marilyn was onto my ruse. One Wednesday night after the church meal, we were talking about something I was struggling with, probably Jay's salvation or finances or parenting. We went into a classroom off the fellowship room where the dinner was served. It was set up for a small group, and Bible story posters and timelines covered the walls.

We sat down, then she turned to me, gently took my hands in hers, bowed her head, and said, "Let's pray." Then to my horror, she added, "You go first."

It was as if my heart was in my throat. Why was I so afraid to speak to the loving heavenly Father she had been teaching me about for so many weeks now? I felt sick, nervous to the point of physical weakness.

If I don't speak, will she just pray for me? What should I do? What should I say?

Marilyn let the silence hang. She wasn't being mean; quite the opposite. She knew I needed to break through this fear and was prodding me to pour out my heart to the only One who could change whatever circumstance I was dealing with.

After what seemed like an eternity, my mouth finally opened. I'm not sure what words came out; they were mostly stifled by sobs anyway, but something fantastic happened. I learned to pray! It would take a lot more practice before I would be comfortable speaking aloud to the Lord, but this first time was the key that unlocked my bondage. Satan wanted me to be silent. Afraid. But being able to openly go to the throne of my heavenly Father gave me—broken, hurting, undereducated me—the freedom to go directly to the source of all power and grace.

When I finished, she squeezed my hand.

"Was that so hard?" she asked with a kind laugh.

"It *is* hard for me to pray out loud with other people," I confessed.

"One thing that helped me was to pray out loud even when I was alone. I got used to hearing my own voice talking to the Lord."

That's weird. But when I tried it, it worked! For one thing, it helped me stay focused. And awake. I eventually became comfortable praying with Marilyn and others, learning to always say a prayer "right where you are" for all occasions. I found that if I promised to pray but didn't stop right then, life got in the way and I'd forget. So I got in the habit instead of always praying right when I learned of the prayer need.

Another important lesson Marilyn instilled in me was the significance of seasons. She taught me that there would be people who came and went through the seasons of my life. Some would be fleeting encounters that I needed to help me grow or learn, and others would be lifelong relationships. She wanted to be sure I understood this so that if there ever came a time that the Lord took her out of my life, or any other person for that matter, that I would not be hurt, wondering why they were gone.

This truth would help me navigate relationships in the years to come. I learned to enjoy the time I had with each person the Lord put in my life and to live fully present in every season.

This season included a new friend named Kim, who like Nikki, also showed me that believers could have fun. I had thought that becoming a Christian meant taking on a boring life. But that wasn't true. Oh, how we laughed! We would act downright childish at times—food fights and silly stories and girlish giggling. Turned out you didn't need to party or drink or smoke to have fun.

Each of the ladies God placed in my life in those early years had such different roles and personalities. We were all at the same church, but they each poured into me differently. Yet they had one thing in common—Marilyn and Kim and Nikki were clearly called to live in a different kind of way. I could tell by watching them interact with others that they were true believers. I learned that though the Holy Spirit was the cleanser of my soul, these good godly friends who prayed with me, encouraged me, and held me accountable were priceless gifts in my new walk with Christ.

Not long after I gave my heart to Jesus, Kim invited me to my first women's conference—Feminar. I had never been to a women's event—not a Christian event anyway—so I had no idea what to expect. When February rolled around, we carpooled to the Macedonia Baptist Church and flowed in through the wide doorways with several hundred other ladies. The air was charged with energy as a band called Selah took the stage and started into an upbeat worship song. All around me, women sang out in a single, strong voice. It was a new experience for me, but I knew this Jesus now, so I could add my voice to the chorus with grateful authenticity.

After the music, the founder of the conference, Janet White, took the stage. What she taught that weekend was about biblical intimacy with your husband and the importance of keeping intimacy pure but vibrant. I'm not sure what I'd expected, but it wasn't this! *Wait, we can talk about sex in church?* I'm not sure how I thought Christian babies were made, but I didn't think Christians had sex—at least not to enjoy it.

When I was able to finally pick up my jaw off the ground, I learned that not only did Christian women have sex, but that they were supposed to enjoy it and initiate it as part of being a godly wife. Janet had such a classy, gentle way of encouraging Christian women to enjoy the beautiful, God-given gift of sexual intimacy within the confines of marriage. She taught us the difference between how men and women respond to intimacy and the importance of keeping our marriages alive and protected. And she gave real details on how to spice up our sex lives. Like a dry sponge, I soaked up each drop of spiritual truth she shared. For the first time in my life, I began to understand that sex was not intended to hurt or destroy and that it was not dirty. Given my history, this was life changing.

After Feminar, I had so many questions. I was beginning to realize how many misconceptions I had of my new faith. That night, Kim and I sat in our hotel room and began to talk. She allowed me the freedom to ask pretty much any question I had. I had no clue how a Christian should act. How a Christian wife should act. How a Christian mom should act. Now I was surrounded by women who freely set examples for me and seemed eager to invest in my life. Kim openly shared her heart. We laughed, we cried, and an unbreakable bond was created that night. Kim became my faithful prayer partner, and I had a feeling that this would be one of those relationships that transcended seasons.

I came away from Feminar with a clear call-to-action from the Lord on the topic of intimacy with my husband: *You need to tell Jay your story.* If only it were that easy.

Chapter 15

Salvation and Secrets

Jay was still not a believer, so I was dead set on getting him saved! To be honest, I was scared for his life. Not his immediate life, but his eternal life. I knew now that he was lost and needed Jesus. I wanted to share with him this new life I'd discovered, even if it meant force-feeding him the gospel. Not surprisingly, that didn't work.

"I don't know what to do about Jay," I confided to Nikki. "How can I make him see that he needs Jesus?"

Nikki smiled. "Do you remember how we engaged with you before you came to church?"

I nodded. "Yeah . . . I guess if you'd been pushy, I would have been turned off."

"Exactly. You need to just love him. Show him Jesus in your actions, and keep praying that God will change his heart. I'll be praying for him too."

Easier said than done. I'd grown used to taking charge in my life. I wasn't going to give up that easily.

"Will you come to church with me?" I asked Jay that night, for the umpteenth time.

"Yeah, okay. I can meet you there in the morning."

"Really, you'll come?"

"I'll be there. I promise."

But on Sunday morning, Jay didn't show. I called him after the service was over, feeling angry and hurt.

"Where are you?" I asked with an edge in my voice.

"I decided to go work on the waterfall," he said. Jay was a stonemason and had been commissioned to build a water feature at the teahouse.

"I'm coming over," I responded, and hung up.

Driving over, I was fuming mad, and I poured out my frustrations to the Lord.

God, I don't want to be mad at my husband, but he lied to me. He let me down!

A still, small voice. *You don't? Are you sure?*

I paused and took a deep breath. I *did* want to be mad. I wanted to chew Jay out!

You're right. I'm sorry. I don't want to want to be mad at him. I need You to change my heart.

Instantly this creepy-cool calm washed over me—a peace that was not humanly possible. I got goosebumps. By the time I pulled into the teahouse, my heart had changed completely.

He had a look of dread on his face when he saw me, no doubt expecting a blowout. But instead of yelling at him and putting him down or criticizing him, I walked over and gave him a hug.

"I just wanted to see you. How's the waterfall coming?"

His expression said, "Who is this woman, and what have you done with my wife?" Instead of asking it though, he motioned to the project and began describing his progress.

This was, perhaps, the first time I showed Jay unwarranted favor and respect. I had never known you could show your husband respect if he didn't earn it. Yet Marilyn had taught me that God's Word instructed me to respect my husband even when I didn't feel he deserved it, just as the Bible instructed him to love me even when I wasn't so loveable. And I certainly hadn't been loveable for most of our marriage. Before Christ, I was downright mean. I taunted Jay when he didn't live up to my standards, belittled him, and reminded him often that I didn't need him. I kept dancing at the club, yet put him down by saying things like, "What kind of a man allows his wife to sell her body on a stage?" I was awful. I did about anything I could to make him prove he was like all the other men in my life, but day after day, blow up after blow up, he continued to love me. He was an amazing dad, always loving my two children who were not biologically his equally as much as he loved Alex.

Jay didn't know Jesus, but he had still loved me far better than I had loved him. Now I knew that my respect for Jay and his love for me shouldn't be dependent on my actions or his. We were to love and respect each other because God commanded us to. I wanted to change Jay, but what I really needed was for God to keep changing me.

After a few minutes, he tentatively asked, "How was church?"

I kept my tone light. "Great! Maybe you can come next time."

He did come the next time. And he kept coming. Jay had come from a family of believers and could answer all the questions of how to be saved, but like me, he hadn't been a true follower of Jesus. As my circle of friends changed, he met more and more of these same Jesus-loving friends and began to see true Christianity being lived out in real time. They loved him as they had loved me—right where he was at spiritually.

When Jay began to go to church and hang around true believers who were amazing and fun and real, he realized he was missing something. As I began to lose some of my crazy and started doing marriage God's way, loving Jay as Christ had instructed me to, he began to see a difference, and that made him curious about getting his own life right with God. He'd been sober for a year, and I think that was part of God's plan. He had given Jay a clear mind so that he could come to know Him in truth.

We headed to church one Sunday, as was our new normal. I went to Sunday school with the kids, and Jay met me for the main service. At the end of the service, the invitation music began for the altar call. We stood in a pew near the back of the room, eyes closed, heads bowed, along with everyone else. Well, eyes mostly closed. I could feel the tension emanating from Jay and couldn't help peeking. His knuckles were turning white from his grip on the back of the pew in front of us.

Could this be the day? *Please, God, make Yourself real to Jay just as You did for me. Show him he needs You.* Time seemed to stand still. There was a slight movement beside me, and suddenly Jay had released his grip to make his own trip down the aisle to surrender his life to Christ.

There wasn't a dry eye in church that morning. The celebration from all my new friends who had been praying so faithfully must have mimicked the celebration in heaven as the angels rejoiced at his acceptance of Christ.

"What made you know you needed to be saved?" I asked Jay after church.

"I left the house this morning fully convinced I was heaven bound on judgment day," he confessed. "I have no clue what the sermon was about, but the Holy Spirit must have been doing something. I suddenly realized, standing there, that I was headed to hell if I didn't accept Jesus."

I hugged him, so grateful that I would get to spend not only my earthly life with this amazing man but an eternity with him and Jesus.

Once Jay and I were both believers, God began to do mighty works in both of us. Our marriage began to change radically. We began to love each other in a way that's only possible with the love of Jesus. I was being mentored and poured into, and I was all in. If this was how the Lord told me to treat my husband, I didn't want to hold anything back. I showed him kindness and stopped saying mean things. I prayed for him and, more importantly, prayed for myself to change. And God was faithful. He began to change me.

But something else changed too. I'm not sure how or when it began, but I started to feel uncomfortable around Jay. Why was I cringing when he walked by and touched my shoulder? Why did I feel scared when we were together in a dark room?

Except for that one drunken night long ago, Jay had never been mean to me, threatened me, or hurt me physically. So where were this tension and fear coming from? Memories of past abuse surfaced with surprising force. Why were they haunting me again? Jay wasn't like any of those men. He loved me. He was good. He was safe.

I thought I had buried all this ugly the day I was baptized, the day the disgusting things had been washed away. But now I was feeling like a scared, grungy child. I hadn't felt this gross since I was a little girl, and it made no sense. For months it continued to get worse. Smells would penetrate my memories, and a monster would be on top of me. My dad would have a "lesson" to teach me. Nightmares attacked my sleep. It was affecting my intimacy with Jay. I remembered the words the Lord had spoken to me at Feminar.

You need to tell him about your past. The secrets I'd kept for years had become a heavy burden. But I didn't want to acknowledge, remember, or talk about any of this. Especially not with my husband. This was in my past. I was clean.

God, I can't tell him. He won't understand.

Again, that voice. *Tell him.*

But what will Jay think? He'll feel betrayed. Trapped. There's just too much.

Trust Me. Tell him.

I pushed back the persistent voice. I was convinced that Jay would leave if he knew all the truth. There it was—my greatest fear: being unwanted. Rejected. Abandoned.

Tell him.

I collapsed into a heap on the floor. *Okay! I'll tell him. If he leaves, I will trust that You are enough. I believe that You want me.*

It took me several weeks to garner the courage, but the day of reckoning finally came. I asked my neighbor Betty Crim to watch the kids for the evening. When Jay walked in the door after a long day at work, I said, "We need to talk."

He looked at me with concern but followed me to sit on the couch. I could barely breathe. Tears quickly overwhelmed the emotional barrier I'd thought I had firmly in place. I was convinced that he would leave when he knew how disgusting I was, when he knew everything I had done and all that had been done to me. *What would he say?*

I could hardly speak over the sobs, but somehow I managed to spill my story. Jay sat in stunned silence, probably not sure how to react. He didn't interrupt—he just listened with more love and compassion than I knew existed. When my sobs finally subsided, I couldn't look at him.

My husband gently tipped my chin up and looked directly into my eyes. "Billy Jo, I love you. This doesn't change anything about the way I feel about you. You're safe, and I'm here for you."

Pure love was all I could see. Then he pulled me into an embrace. Held me so close, so tight. He wasn't repulsed.

"Of course I forgive you," he whispered into my hair. "Though I don't feel like you need my forgiveness. Those things that were done to you weren't your fault. And you know I'm not perfect either."

We both had ugly in our past. The only difference was that I had known most of his before I married him.

Our marriage changed again that day. It was as if the love I had feared losing had multiplied instead. As soon as my obedience and trust in the Lord took over and I told Jay everything, the Lord lifted those uncontrollable responses to innocent interactions that had begun to paralyze me months before. The fears and nightmares stopped. Occasionally the dark memories would trigger, but they didn't control me anymore. I could speak truth into my own heart and mind to make those moments pass in seconds. Bit by bit, God was healing my heart.

Chapter 16

A New Father

Alex, now four years old and my squeaky little chatterbox, started talking even before she got into the car.

"Are you buckled?" I asked, interrupting the flow of chatter once she had climbed into her seat. I heard the click of the seat belt.

"Yes!"

Alex had spent the weekend with my in-laws, Austin was with his dad, and Ashlei was with Jackie, giving Jay and me a blessed break from parenting. I waved as we pulled out of the driveway, smiling at the stream of sentences that continued from the backseat. Alex rattled on about everything she could think of, when unexpectedly she took me aback.

"Mommy, is your daddy still alive?"

I hadn't had contact with my father for several years. I gripped the steering wheel and took a breath.

"Alex, I really don't know."

"Well, don't you think you should find out?" She was so matter of fact.

"You're probably right." I was flabbergasted. *Where on earth did this come from?* My mind quickly worked to divert the conversation. "Tell me more about your weekend."

Alex happily picked up where she'd left off. My mind wasn't so easily sidetracked. The last time I'd seen my father was . . . well, I couldn't really remember. I couldn't pinpoint a time when I'd cut off our relationship; it just kind of happened. There was no intentional goodbye. I think I simply decided I was done and never went back to see him and stopped calling. It hurt less to move forward.

That afternoon, as I stood in the laundry room transferring clean clothes from the washer to the dryer, my phone rang. I checked the caller ID. It was my father. I stared at the screen, shocked. *Alex just asked about him this morning. This is too weird. Why is he calling me? Should I answer?*

I only had a few more rings to make a decision. I hesitantly punched the Call button to pick up.

"Hello?"

My dad's broken voice came across the line. "Billy Jo?"

"Yes, it's me."

"I wasn't sure you would answer my call."

Silence.

A moment later he began again, clearly emotional. "Billy Jo, I've lived a terrible life. I've done terrible things—to you, to everyone. I am so sorry. Will you forgive me?"

Sobs overtook the conversation. My mind raced. I thought of those last days with my mother, when I'd found it in my heart to forgive her, even before I knew the forgiveness of Christ. Now I knew the depths of His forgiveness toward me. He'd freed me from the pain and bondage of my father's abuse. After I got saved, God had freed me from the emotional desire to have an earthly dad that would love me. I no longer craved the acceptance of my father because I had a heavenly Father who was perfect. Now, I had the opportunity to extend His forgiveness.

"Dad, of course I forgive you," I whispered once his sobs subsided.

"If it's not too late, I want to know my grandkids. I want a relationship with you. Is there any chance I can take you out to dinner?" His relief was evident in his voice.

"Yes, I'd like that."

"How about tonight?"

"I'll check with Jay, but that should work."

We made a quick plan to meet, and I hung up, stunned at what had just happened. I thought again of Alex's probing question this morning.

"I guess he is alive," I said softly to myself.

That night, Jay and I met my dad and his girlfriend, Pat, at a local restaurant. When I'd confessed my past to Jay, I hadn't told him who any of my abusers were. He hadn't pushed me for details, so he probably didn't know one was my father. Jay only knew I didn't have a relationship with my father, and he'd left it at that. Now, here we were walking into a restaurant to have dinner together.

My dad and Pat were already at a table. They stood to greet us, and the tears in my father's eyes mirrored my own. My dad hugged me tightly, and I didn't pull away. For the first time in my life, I felt the love from him I had always craved. He shook hands with Jay, and Pat gave me a warm hug, introducing herself. She looked different from most of the women my dad had dated. She looked grandmotherly, not sleazy old lady—which was more his usual type.

Dad looked around for my children and was clearly disappointed they hadn't come along, but he didn't say anything more than ask where they were and didn't press me for an explanation. Conversation was light. We didn't talk about the past. I found out my father was living in a small camper on Lake Tyler. He'd been experiencing health problems but nothing too serious. We talked; we laughed; we healed.

My dad was not yet saved, but it was clear the Lord was after his heart. There were too many changes in him for it to be anything but God. Over the next few months, we had many meals and visits together. Slowly and very much supervised, he began to visit and get to know my children. I even went with him to his doctor appointments.

But I always chickened out when there were opportunities to share the gospel with him. I didn't know if I feared he would reject me or the Lord, but I just couldn't do it.

One day I got a call from his girlfriend.

"BJ, your dad's in the hospital. It doesn't look good, and you need to come as soon as possible. You're his only next of kin, and they need your permission to treat him."

I arrived, emotional, assuming the worst. Pat met me in the waiting room and led me to the front desk.

"They're waiting to take him into surgery. Here, sign these papers."

I scribbled my name, and we sat down together in the waiting room.

"What happened?" I asked.

"I didn't hear from your dad for three days, and that isn't like him, so I went over and forced the door open. I found him motionless on the floor, greenish in color. I called 911, and they sent an ambulance. I still don't know what's wrong with him."

Dad was in surgery for hours. The surgeon finally came out to report that he was stable but not out of danger. His intestines had burst, and for three days he had lain with waste in his abdomen.

"We cleaned all we could, but we had to remove most of his intestines. We put in a colostomy bag."

"When can we see him?"

"He should be awake for visitors in a few hours," the doctor replied.

After Dad's surgery, I called my pastor and asked him if he would visit my dad. I explained he wasn't saved. Brother Tom went to see him that night and clearly presented the gospel. My dad wept—more than Brother Tom had ever witnessed a grown man weep. Maybe it was because he shouldn't have lived, and he knew it. What mattered was that my dad chose to cry out to Jesus and ask Him to forgive him of all his sins. He had been cruel, abusive, and quite honestly, disgusting for most of his life. Yet he committed his life to the Lord that night and found grace and redemption.

A New Father

I had the great privilege to watch my dad be transformed over the next three years before cancer won the battle and claimed his life. His entire countenance changed after his salvation. He was forgiven, and his life showed this in his behavior. His speech became pure. He was loving and gentle. He would still have an occasional beer, but rarely. Before, he had hated God and anything to do with God. Now, I was able to share stories of my friends and my job and our church, and he listened intently. We shared daily phone calls that usually ended with an "I love you." Hugs that didn't feel dirty. Conversations where he was interested to learn who I was, who my children were, and what we liked. We went on camping trips where we laughed and roasted weenies and made s'mores over an open campfire. We spent holidays together. He and Austin, now twelve, became close. Eventually, I would trust him to take Austin fishing, and this became a regular outing for the two of them.

Time. Time was our only item of value, and he gave as much of it to us as he could. With his health and stamina low, he could not bear much, so our visits were short but often. Toward the end, he was too ill to attend church, but he was saved, and the Lord of the universe had changed my dad from the inside out. I wish I could go back and tell my childhood self how this would all turn out. Who would have thought this relationship could be redeemed? Only God.

Chapter 17

Call to Ministry

We'd been a faithful, churchgoing family for nearly two years when a need arose in student ministries. Somehow, I was put on the search committee. After many temper tantrums and arguments with the Lord, the new youth director ended up being *me*! Me, teaching young people about Jesus? Only God would do something like that. When I started, there were exactly three students who attended regularly. But God grew it into a thriving youth ministry of nearly forty teenagers. When another youth group invited us to join them at summer camp, I jumped at the opportunity. I had no clue what was required to take a group to summer camp, but I felt it was important to take my students, so off we went. I might have been an adult, but for the first time in my life, I got to go to youth camp, and boy, was it fun!

One night the chapel speaker gave an invitation, and students flocked to the altar. The Lord was working strongly. As I sat there praying, someone tapped my shoulder. I looked up, and they summoned me to counsel some of the students wishing to give their lives to Christ. Talk about panic! It was like when Marilyn first made me pray out loud, but a bazillion times worse. I'd never led anyone to Christ, and I had no clue what to do. What to say. *What if I screw this up?* I made my way to the corner to speak with a young girl.

Despite my fear, God gave me the words to speak to her, and she did indeed give her life to Christ and accept Him as her Savior. Camp was a life-changing week for both of us.

I knew for certain the Lord had called me into ministry, but I still struggled with what that meant and what that would look like. At camp I was surrounded by so many role models and awesome examples of great youth leaders, and I wanted to be just like them—all of them. I wanted to be great, and I battled with the Lord over this. What the Lord was calling me to be was *me*—a saved, redeemed me. I realized I wasn't sure how well I could pull that off. I had so much baggage. But I discovered how freeing it was when I stopped trying to imitate other people's style and allowed the Lord to develop His style in me. It was after I surrendered to this teaching from the Lord that He began blessing the youth ministry.

Around the same time, my friends encouraged me to go back to school. *Don't they remember—I dropped out of high school! Now they think I should go to college?* I was way too old to even consider that. But my friends kept nudging me, until I finally picked up the phone and called the Baptist Missionary Association Theological Seminary in Jacksonville, Texas. Expecting to make an appointment for some time in the next month or so, I was shocked when the receptionist made the appointment for the next day for me to talk to the dean of students.

Satan's voice whispered, *You're not ready. It's stupid to even go talk to them.* I assumed there was no way they would accept me, but I had promised my friends I would go, so I did. After all, it was only to find out if I had any chance to go there and to see what was required for acceptance. I spent hours getting ready for the meeting—hair as perfect as I could get it, makeup just right, my best skirt and blouse. Then I headed to the seminary.

The dean was very kind. He walked me through all my options and informed me how to accomplish all I needed to do.

"Do you have any questions?" he asked when he had finished.

"Yes, is there a dress code?" As an insecure woman, I didn't want to wear the wrong clothes!

"It's pretty casual. Women should wear dresses or skirts while attending classes. What you're wearing today would be fine."

What I'm wearing today is casual? These are my fancy clothes, mister!

Thankfully, God gave me enough grace to keep my mouth poised in a nice smile. I thanked him for his time and left, nearly in tears. I was wearing my only skirt, a long brown flowy suede that was a hand-me-down from a friend. At home, I spilled all the details to my precious friend Betty Crim, who was now more like a spiritual mother. She was so excited for me, so encouraging.

All I could think was *I can't go . . . I'll be expected to wear church clothes every day!* There was no way I could buy more clothes suitable for me to adhere to the dress code, so I prepared my heart to be done with this dream. At least at that point. I didn't expect to be accepted anyhow, so there was no need to worry over clothes I wouldn't even need.

To my surprise, I was accepted into seminary. Days before my first class, Betty took me shopping for new clothes. After taking me to lunch, she bought me a whole new wardrobe. I had never had new school clothes growing up. Maybe a new item here or there, but certainly not an entire wardrobe. At first I was uncomfortable, but the joy she took in gifting it to me made me have fun too.

That day made me feel wanted and that I had value. I didn't miss the metaphor. New clothes perfectly represented my new identity in Christ. The stained rags of abuse, abortions, drugs—He'd taken them upon Himself at Calvary and had instead given me a clean garment of grace. Even as special and loved as I felt shopping that day, it didn't compare to how special I was in God's eyes. The Lord called me His chosen one, beloved, set apart, His friend. It was still a hard concept for me to hold tight to.

Just as I started seminary, God called Jay and me to serve at another church in our area. Leaving my student ministry was a difficult transition. I loved those kids more than I dreamed possible! I continued working at the teahouse, but eventually I knew the Lord was telling me to let go of that too. What a leap of faith that took! During my four years at seminary, I served as a youth director at our new church. I was quite proud that I made the dean's list three semesters and graduated summa cum laude with a 4.0 GPA! As I was about to complete my college degree, I felt the Lord moving us once again. Just before graduation, we began searching for a new church home, and I learned of a local church needing a youth pastor.

"You know, as a woman you'll never have a paying job in a southern Baptist church," one of my youth director colleagues told me. "Women can be Sunday school teachers, children's workers, nursery workers, and secretaries."

He was a dear friend, but his words scared me. Had I gone to seminary for nothing? Would my career in youth ministry be limited? Fortunately, God's plans were bigger than my friend could have imagined.

I applied for the youth pastor position anyway but had the most horrible interview imaginable. I mean, it was awful! Basically, I spent two hours explaining why I was underqualified and completely the wrong person for the job. I rambled on and on and, in no shortage of words, explained that my church was awesome and I really didn't want to leave it. I don't know why I was verbally throwing up for two hours in this man's office, but the pastor was kind, and when I finally shut my mouth, he began to tell me, in love, everything I'd done wrong in that time. He clearly told me that he saw potential in me and gave me some great pointers.

He also told me a few other things that at the moment I didn't like; however, he spoke great truths. He told me that if I truly desired to serve in full-time ministry, I had to get okay with taking a paycheck. Obviously I knew I needed to be paid, but I struggled with the fear of doing ministry for a paycheck. My heart was not and had never been about the money. I wanted to be a difference-maker.

Call to Ministry

He also told me that if I desired to make a career in full-time ministry, I had to be willing to leave my church. Truth was, my church was dying; it was full of wonderful people, but they were not given much to do for the kingdom. This made me mad. I loved my church. And though I knew the Lord was telling me to move on, I wasn't happy about it.

The last thing he shared with me was that if a church saw potential in someone and really desired to have them on staff, they would create a position for them. He ended by encouraging me to go home, get my act together, and come back. If for no other reason than to prove to this man that I was not a complete buffoon, I did make another appointment. And I brought it! Unfortunately, they hired another person, but he began to mentor me despite the fact that I was a stranger and not one of his members. He gave me people to contact and encouraged me in many ways.

As we began searching for a new church home, I really wanted to try his church, Flint Baptist Church, first. Jay and I knew pretty quickly that this was where the Lord was calling us. We began attending and serving, and eventually, true to his word, the pastor created a new position, Mission and Ministries Director, and offered it to me. What started out as a volunteer position ultimately became a paid staff job—and one that wasn't limited to the list my friend had drawn for women in ministry. I was a bit confused as to why God would have me go through four years of studying to be a youth director just to change my heart and my direction, but I soon discovered that the Lord had perfectly designed a job that I absolutely adored.

In my new job, I was the church liaison for all our ministries and missions inside and outside our church. I served on several boards of directors, which helped me to stay in the loop of all that the ministries were doing and what their needs were. I helped get church members plugged in to different ministries and mission opportunities and helped develop new opportunities within our church.

Another key responsibility of my job was managing the community benevolence needs. Oh, the irony! Knowing how I had felt most of my life about approaching the church for help, God had a sense of humor in that. Now when people needed help, the little girl who had been dragged in and out of churches begging for money was the one people came to. Because of my experience, I could identify the telltale signs of people abusing the benevolence system. I heard the same words my own mother had used so many times, the lies, the deception, and the shenanigans people would pull just to get an electric bill paid. I used great discernment when having these talks, but I was often blunt, especially for individuals who came often but did nothing to change their circumstances. But for those who really needed help and whose efforts were in good faith, I found great joy in helping with their needs.

I had come full circle, and I loved life serving in full-time ministry.

Chapter 18

Sharing My Story

I sank into the leather couch in the church administration office and looked over at my friend Connie.

"Okay, tell me more about this idea of yours."

I met weekly with Connie to disciple her. We shared life together and sought to solve all the world's problems as we processed through life challenges, prayed, studied God's Word, and memorized Scripture. Connie had recently joined the program-planning team at our church. She pulled out a piece of cardboard.

"I was thinking we could have people do a cardboard testimony and write their sin on one side, like *adultery*, or *abortion*, or *drug addict*, and then flip it over and write something like *forgiven*, *redeemed*, or *sober*."

"That sounds good," I said.

"Oh, and I want to kick off the project by having you tell your story. It could be really powerful."

I gulped. I had only told Jay and a handful of close friends about my past. Connie knew my story because our mentoring relationship required us to be real and vulnerable, but my story wasn't public knowledge by any means.

"I'll pray about it," I told her, since that is what mature, spiritual, Jesus-loving ladies did—but in truth, I had no intention of ever getting on that stage and telling my story. I was on staff at one of our town's most prosperous and growing churches. Get up in front of the congregation? I simply couldn't do it.

But I did pray about it, as I'd promised. My prayer went something like this: *Lord, You know what will happen if I do this, so You know I simply cannot do it. There is too much ugliness. Too much brokenness. Too much pain. Too much sin. So thanks, but no thanks. Amen.*

Never mind that I had clearly heard a new call from the Lord at Feminar this year. *You will be a speaker telling your story—My story.*

I brushed off the nudge I felt from the Holy Spirit. Instead, I told Connie that I didn't feel like I should be the one to speak. Translated, I was really saying, *There is no way I have enough faith or courage to get on a stage with hundreds and hundreds of people listening and staring at me and tell them all my junk. A group of strangers maybe, but not here with people who know me. Not at my church where I also serve on staff.*

Connie was disappointed. "BJ, I really feel the Lord saying you are supposed to be the speaker, but I know you well enough to know that you have covered this in prayer, and I trust you and respect your decision."

Right about then I hid in the shadow of my boulder of shame, because I knew I had deceived her. I was afraid. And she was correct—I was the one who was supposed to speak that night, but in fear, I refused to do so.

With that discussion over, she continued to plan, and I continued to be disobedient. The closer the night of the program came, the more I knew I was supposed to speak. But still, I remained silent, stuck in fear. Besides, she already had another person scheduled, and it wasn't like I could say, "Okay, I'm in—I'm your girl. I'll do it!" Now it was too late.

The night arrived, and I sat in the audience, fully aware that I should have been backstage preparing to speak. Instead, an amazingly brave, clearly faith-filled woman who had overcome a massive drug addiction shared her story. It was a beautiful example of Christ's amazing, redeeming, life-saving love, but I knew it was supposed to be me up there sharing my story. I became physically ill and had to text Connie and apologize right then, confessing to her that she was right and that, basically, I was a big fat chicken, too scared to be obedient to the call to share my story. Sitting in that pew in that moment, I cried out to God and said, *Lord, if You ever give me another chance to tell my story and all You rescued me from, I promise I will never say no again.*

Two weeks later I was helping with our annual Ladies Salad Supper and was assigned to host our guest speaker—none other than Feminar founder Janet White. All my friends knew that Janet was my hero, which is why I landed this "job." I dissolved into a fangirl as I sat down to dinner next to my very own spiritual mentor.

Within minutes of our meeting, she began to ask me about myself. *Janet White wants to know about me?* In the few moments we had before she got up to pour spiritual truths and challenges into our walk with Jesus, I gave her a short synopsis of my story, telling her why I loved Feminar so much and how her teaching had impacted me personally.

Just before she got up to go on stage, she said, "BJ, I think I am supposed to have you share your story at Feminar this year." And then— gracefully—as only Janet White can, she delivered a Billy Graham– worthy message in her gentle and inspiring way.

Janet took my phone number at the end of the night. I was flattered that she wanted me to share my story, but Feminar was nine months away, and I assumed it would blow over and be forgotten. The next day, Janet sent me the kindest text, thanking me for sharing my story with her and telling me that she would be in touch about Feminar. The text sent me over the moon in excitement. I took a screenshot of the message and sent it to my closest friends as proof that I, B. J. Garrett, had gotten a personal message from Janet White! I was quite ridiculous.

Janet made good on her word. I was sitting in the same office where I had declined the invitation to share my story with a few hundred of my own church members when I received a text from Janet, asking me when I could meet to film a video for Feminar. The Lord had given me another chance!

This time, in front of approximately 2,300 women, mine would be the highlighted story for that year's conference. Filming that video was like a movie-star moment with Jesus. The day she sent me the link to the video, I was nervous to even click on it, but I watched in awe at how the film guy had turned my ugly story into a beautiful picture of hope and salvation through Jesus. I also panicked. This was actually happening.

When I had promised during that program at church to never say no again, I had not dreamed that meant anything this huge. I was terrified. Still, no one knew my story—not my family (besides Jay), not my church, not even my pastor, who was also my dear friend and boss. And it was about to be out there for all to see.

I decided a few key people should see it before it aired at Feminar, like my pastor and his wife, my mother-in-law, and a few other important people in my life. I didn't want them to be blindsided with such personal sin and trauma at the conference. They offered nothing but love and support after viewing it. No shame or condemnation, just love. I tried to get Ashlei to watch it, but she refused, saying she wanted to watch it for the first time when it played at Feminar. She assured me there was nothing in that video that would make her love me less.

The day arrived, and Janet called me on stage as they rolled the video. Standing on that Belcher Center stage and seeing the fulfillment of what the Lord had told me would come to pass, I was emotional and overwhelmed with God's grace in my life. I was living a dream I hadn't even had the faith to dream or the courage to believe. I stood there looking out over the thousands of burgundy theater-style seats filled with women, and it was amazing. That the Lord would allow such a broken, sin-filled, damaged woman like me to share about His redemptive power and grace filled me with awe.

Afterward, I heard the Lord say to me, *This is just the beginning. You will write a book, and I will get all the glory.* In tears I accepted the calling, knowing I wasn't a writer. Knowing I was more afraid at that moment than probably any other moment in my life. But if He could do this, if He could make something beautiful out of my disgusting sin, then how could I deny Him? He had saved me from so much. I had to accept. I knew that if I refused to obey, if I refused to write my story, then another would take my place. If I stayed silent, "even the stones would cry out" (Luke 19:40).

So I began.

Chapter 19

On a Mission

"Have a safe trip," I said as Jay fastened a luggage tag onto his bag outside the airport security line.

He stood up when he finished and pulled me into a hug.

"I'll be praying for the results of your CT scan. I wish I could be there with you."

I had begun to have some health problems a few months earlier. At first the doctor had considered multiple sclerosis, but once that had been ruled out, the next guess was possibly a cancerous tumor in my thymus. I didn't even know what a thymus was, but the word *cancer* had struck fear into my heart. I'd lost both of my parents to cancer. Would my fate be the same?

Now, on the day of my test, Jay was leaving for Cuba on a mission trip with our church, and we wouldn't have contact for eight days. Once Jay left Florida, he would "go dark," with no communication for the duration of his time there, until he landed back on US soil. We were both going dark—him by way of technology, me by way of the CT machine. We were scared.

I watched him make his way through security. He gave me one

last wave before he disappeared down the corridor toward the gates. I turned and headed toward my destination—the doctor's office. The CT scan took only moments, and I didn't have to wait long for the results. The next day, the doctor called me with good news. I didn't have cancer! My health complications were due to an autoimmune disorder.

If only I could tell Jay . . .

I went into work and bebopped my way upstairs to my office at the church, full of joy and relief in knowing that I didn't have cancer. The red light flashing on my phone announced a voicemail, and I clicked the Speaker button. The familiar voice of Danny Pickens, the Smith Baptist Association's Director of Missions, came onto the line.

"Hi, BJ. We're planning a mission trip to Uganda, and the Lord has laid on my heart that you should lead the women's team. I'd love to discuss this further with you, so please give me a call back."

Me? Lead a mission trip?

Jay had gone on mission trips to Cuba for several years now, but I hadn't, mostly because Alex was too young for us both to travel out of the country. To be honest, I didn't want to travel anywhere. Just the idea of travel stirred up feelings of insecurities from my transient childhood. My dream had always been to have a house and live in it forever.

But my heart toward travel began to change after a few years of Jay going to Cuba. I was starting to resent him going without me, serving in missions and leaving us home. One year I was so hurt by feeling like he was leaving us that I messaged an old boyfriend. The second I sent the message on social media, the Lord slapped some sense into my heart, and I immediately deleted it. But in my heart, I had crossed a very dangerous line.

Even as a Jesus-loving woman in ministry, my heart was deceitful. The Enemy was always waiting and watching for me to be weak and insecure and hurting. Had it not been for the Lord's interception that night, I might have done the unthinkable, and I am not sure our marriage would have survived it. And all while my husband was doing kingdom work! When he came home, I confessed to him where my heart had almost taken me.

Now that Alex was older, maybe my time for missions had come. There was just one problem: I didn't have a passport. Yes—I was the missions director of a church, and I didn't have a passport.

I called Danny back, thanking him profusely for considering me, and sheepishly explained my dilemma. If he was appalled that I didn't have a passport, he didn't let it show.

"No problem. The trip isn't until October, so you have plenty of time to get your passport. When Jay gets home, you two pray about it, talk to Pastor Sam, and get back to me."

I hung up from that call with growing excitement. It felt good to even be considered! Would God really send me to Africa? Brother Sam seemed to think so. To my great delight and surprise, he thought I would be great leading the women's team and thought I should go; he even offered church funds to get my passport.

But I still couldn't talk to Jay for another week! I began asking God to give me clarity and to prepare Jay's heart to support this crazy idea. Daily I hit my knees, asking for confirmation and discernment about going on this mission trip. I prayed most of all that if indeed I was supposed to go, Jay would think we both should go and serve side by side.

This seemed an outlandish prayer because Jay was already on a trip this year, and I knew his heart was for the people of Cuba. He'd never mentioned going anywhere else. And how would we pay the expenses of two people? What would we do about Alex, our only child still in school and living at home? Ashlei had her hands full caring for two small children on her own, and Austin . . . well, Austin was not even taking very good care of himself at twenty years old. I could not leave Alex with either of them. To even consider the possibility seemed preposterous. But I couldn't stop asking God to send Jay and me to Uganda.

When Jay landed in Florida, he called me immediately. His first words were, "What were the results?"

The results of what? Why are you so panicked?

I'd completely forgotten the cancer scare. That seemed ages ago. I'd had more than a week to know I didn't have cancer and the same amount of time to grow in excitement over this new mission opportunity. But Jay had no idea of any of this. Unbeknownst to me, he'd spent his entire time in Cuba praying for me, worried sick about what health news he would hear when he came home.

"Oh, no cancer!" I said quickly. "But, Jay, I've been asked to go to Uganda on a mission trip! What do you think?"

Jay was stunned. "Billy Jo, you'll never believe this. While I was in Cuba, I decided that I would no longer serve on the mission field without you and prayed for opportunities to serve together."

The Lord had answered both our prayers in a big way. We decided that we would serve together from now on. If one of us was called to go on a mission trip, then both of us would go. We both loved missions, but this decision was as much to protect our marriage as it was about serving. I knew Satan would love nothing more than to destroy our testimony of a God-honoring marriage, so safeguarding that would always be a top priority.

Our trip to Uganda was on. From the first moments we landed, I was in love with this place, with these people.

We landed in Kampala and then headed to Bethany Village, an orphan-filled small peninsula off the shores of Lake Victoria. I swallowed hard as I saw the boats we were to take to Bethany Village. Long, narrow, wooden. Like an overgrown canoe with a canopy at one end. One boat for our entire team. All fifteen of us. We stowed our gear in the sun and crowded ourselves on the narrow seats under the shade. Good thing I knew God was in this trip, because I don't think I'd have gotten aboard without Him. But in we climbed and down the river we went. That forty-five-minute voyage was quite the adventure—we had to bail water the whole way! Nearby, the locals cast nets out of their boats. Along the shore, I caught glimpses of children wearing only shorts— no shoes or shirts. When we docked, they met us with large brown inquisitive eyes. One small boy—Abus—wouldn't leave our side. He held tightly to Jay's hand, then slid his hands up and down our arms, fascinated by our white skin. The local ministry we were partnering with had cautioned us not to make promises we couldn't keep, especially concerning child sponsorships. Most of these children were unable to attend school and didn't have the essentials for daily survival. My heart was heavy for Abus, for all of them. I would have taken them all home if it were possible!

In the following days, we did mercy ministries—packaging beans, rice, lentils, maize flour, and vitamins, and distributing them to families living in the slums. Using downed trees as bridges, we crossed streams of sewage to reach one-room homes with dirt floors and no furniture. The people's hearts were ready to receive the gospel of Jesus Christ as we delivered food for their stomachs as well as food for their souls. So many lives were saved for eternity. It was incredible.

We also held a women's conference, where I spoke. As I had prepared for this trip, I wondered why God had chosen me. I didn't know how these precious women would ever relate to me. Overwhelmed, I watched the parade of women walking up the steep red-clay terrain, women who had walked miles to hear me tell them about the love of Jesus. They began to fill the makeshift benches in the one-room church. It was humbling.

Day one was pretty full. By day two, the word had spread, and the attendance more than doubled. There was standing room only. I shared His story through the details of my life, one phrase at a time, through Ruth, my translator. Despite my insecurities, the Lord used my story in powerful ways to connect with these women.

One woman came up to me afterward, asking for prayer.

"My son is crazy and has abandoned his family. His wife abandoned their children a year ago, and now I have them. Please pray that I don't abandon them also."

She was so fearful and worn out from trying to feed and care for her grandchildren that she was truly considering abandoning them. This wasn't unusual in Uganda; abandoned children were commonplace.

She continued: "Your story of overcoming abandonment made me want to be the woman of God they need."

Feeling unwanted wasn't an emotion unique to me. Maybe here, in rural Africa, I could make one less child feel unwanted. I prayed for this grandmother to have the strength and faith and resources needed to care for her grandchildren. When I finished, we both had tears in our eyes. She laid a withered hand on my arm.

"If God would send a *mzungu*, a white person, all this way just to speak to us, then He must love us."

Our ministry may have touched their lives, but these women changed mine forever.

We also did tent revivals and outreach ministries to share the gospel. Our team was broken up into small groups, each with different assignments. We all served long, hard days, but in the end, hundreds accepted Jesus as their Savior.

After our time of serving ended, we took a two-day safari excursion to unwind and debrief. We saw lions and elephants and all kinds of wildlife. We rode down the Nile, surrounded by hippos. Ironically, our guide was named Moses. I did have an amazing time, but I found it difficult to embrace carefree fun; I couldn't turn off the emotional connection with the people I had poured into for the past ten days. My entire world had been shaken; my heart was now broken for the people of Africa.

I cried for about three months after coming home. I was suddenly sensitive to the waste and spoiledness of our nation. I longed to return to Africa. I had never felt more complete or more alive and in the center of God's will than I did in Uganda. A new love for serving in missions was cemented in my heart.

When the next year came around, my heart for Africa was as strong as ever, but we were both invited to serve in Cuba. I was excited to serve with Jay, but while I knew that he felt toward Cuba as I did toward Africa, in truth I would have preferred to go back to Africa. As we prepared for our trip to Cuba, I held a secret resentment. Why would the

Lord send me to Uganda if He wasn't going to allow me to return? Jay loved Cuba, and I wanted to love Cuba also, but how could my heart be shared with two places?

The moment we made it through customs and into the embrace of those waiting for us, however, I was immediately remorseful. How could I have dreaded this? I was instantly in love with the beautiful faces before me.

The mission work was different in Cuba, but again, I was able to speak to numerous groups of women, sharing my personal story and teaching Scripture while sharing the gospel. Experiencing the faith of the Cuban people was convicting. Their lives couldn't be compared to the lives of those we had served in Africa, but they, too, held to their faith completely. The Lord grew my heart enough for me to love another people group. I had not thought it possible to love another people or place like I loved Africa.

What I loved even more was watching my husband in action and serving with him. He'd been amazing in Africa, but here in Cuba, he was so much more. He was reunited with the people of *his* heart, and it was a beautiful sight. After all those years of staying at home, I got to experience Cuba with him. It took my love for him to new depths. At our wedding all those years ago, I had giggled at the thought of honoring and obeying him. Now, as we served Christ together, I knew what that meant. I hadn't known it was possible to love him this much.

Jay and I continued to return to Cuba, eventually taking Alex with us. Each trip, I walked away even more changed and more in love with our holy Lord. Though I still longed to return to Africa, I was now eager to go wherever God sent me. God taught me a powerful lesson through these mission trips: He could use me as effectively in my own community as He could across continents and countries, *if* I was ready to serve Him. I had a mission field wherever I was.

Chapter 20

CARE

I leaned forward from the plush cushion of the theater seat as the lights came up and the closing credits began to roll. I'd just seen a screening of the movie *October Baby*, the story of a young woman whose world was rocked when she learned she was the adopted survivor of a failed abortion. The guilt of my own abortions surfaced uncomfortably as a woman took the stage in front of the screen.

Dr. Grace English shared about Christ-Centered Abortion Recovery and Education, or CARE, a local nonprofit that existed to restore lives wounded by abortion and to educate the community of its consequences. I was already serving in full-time ministry, but I was intrigued. Maybe my experience could help someone else who was hurting. Afterward, I went up to speak with Dr. Grace, to get more information. I got a card, shoved it deep into my purse, and didn't think about it again—that is, until I stumbled across the CARE booth at a local street fair a few weeks later. Again, I spoke to them, took a card, and did nothing.

A few months later, at Feminar, I watched a testimony video of a woman who'd had several abortions and had found healing through the ministry of CARE. During the break, I stopped by their booth, spoke to Dr. Grace, and took another card. This time, however, I also gave her my number. *Okay, God, I'm starting to get the hint.*

On the way home that weekend, one of the ladies carpooling with our group began talking about the woman in the video. Immediately I became defensive on her behalf, not really knowing why I was so upset. I assumed it was righteous anger for another broken woman. In truth, I was still hurting from my own abortions that I had never dealt with.

After Feminar, I finally called and made an appointment with Dr. Grace. She came to meet me in my church office a few days later.

"What can I do for you?" she asked to start off our conversation.

"Well, I'm fine—I don't need your services—but I would like to learn more so that I can help other women who are hurting."

Grace smiled. "That's nice, but in order to help others through CARE, you'll need to go through the program yourself."

I filled out my paperwork, only acknowledging my first abortion, and signed up to attend a CARE weekend event. When I arrived, I had no idea how much I needed this ministry or the work the Lord would do in my heart.

We went around the table, sharing our stories. I began by telling the story of my first abortion, but when I finished, I just kept talking. I told the group that I had gone again for a second abortion.

"But I wasn't really pregnant; it was a false procedure."

As soon as the words left my mouth, I was stunned. Where did that come from? I had not acknowledged that day since.

With much grace and love, one of the leaders kindly looked me in the eye. "BJ," she said, "I believe the Lord has you here to acknowledge the second child you aborted."

Instantly, my walls went up. I was not prepared for this. This was hard. I went back to my private room, completely broken. The realization of what I had done—not once but twice—hit me with more pain than I knew how to express. I fell to the ground, wailing out to God. It was painful, but it was also healing. Through Bible study, the leading of the Holy Spirit, and the leaders of CARE, I walked away from that weekend fully healed, acknowledging both of the children I had lost through abortion. In true BJ fashion, I was all in.

CARE had so impacted my heart and my life that I knew I had to get more involved. I began volunteering and helping in the kitchen during the weekend studies. In time, I started leading weekend sessions and sharing my story. Eventually, they asked me to serve on the board of directors.

Not everything in my life at this time was going smoothly. I had served as mission director at Flint Baptist Church for about five years, when another ministry that helped teen pregnant moms pursued me to come to work for them as their assistant director. I had fasted and prayed, and with the complete blessing of my church, I accepted the position. It turned out to be a terrible experience.

I learned valuable information, but the job only lasted a short ten months. After losing the position, I swore I would never work in a ministry again. It hurt too much if it went bad. If I had an awful boss who was not a Christian, at least I knew they were lost. But it should have been different with a Christian boss. When a Christian treated people the way I had been treated, it was unacceptable. I didn't ever want to put myself through that again.

So I started looking for another job. I was determined not to apply for ministry positions, but through the mentorship of my pastor's wife and praying friends, however, the Lord confirmed that I would indeed continue in full-time ministry. Yet after a few months, I still had no prospects. We were sinking financially, and I had to get a job. I applied everywhere, including a cookie company. When I couldn't even land a job baking cookies, I was at an all-time low professionally. It was depressing.

One Friday I got a call from a dialysis company with a job offer. It was really good money with great benefits. I would have to work in a cubicle, which sounded miserable. But I needed a job, and I would take what I could get. I vowed to be thankful and to learn all that I could while the Lord had me there.

I accepted the position and then texted my five closest prayer-warrior friends to tell them the news and that I would start on Monday. By mistake I included the board president of CARE. Though we were friends, Jo wasn't in my inner circle. She immediately called me, and in complete honesty, I shared with her that I didn't want this job but felt I had no choice. I had to accept the position. She could probably hear in my voice that I was on the verge of tears. Jo prayed with me and told me to continue praying and assured me that the Lord had a plan.

I was making a grocery run later in the day when she called me back. I didn't usually talk to her that often unless it was for the ministry work of CARE, so I was surprised to see her number on my phone.

"Hello?"

"It's Jo again. BJ, I need you to pray about something . . ."

"Okay?"

"The board and I have been meeting privately about making you a job offer. We've prayed fervently, and we feel you are supposed to be our executive director. We had a meeting planned for Monday to finalize an offer."

She told me what they could offer financially. It was significantly less than the other position I had accepted just hours before, and they couldn't offer benefits. But it didn't matter. There was no question in my mind that this was the answer to my months of prayer. I accepted the position on the spot.

On Monday, I started my new job—not in a cubicle at a dialysis company but as the executive director of the ministry I was already so invested in. There was lots of work to do. In those early weeks, the office was in shambles, in the middle of a major furniture rearrangement. I was hot and tired one day, when my office phone rang. We didn't get many real calls at this point, so I assumed it would be another robot sales call. But I climbed over the piles of office debris anyway and grabbed the phone.

"Good afternoon, Thank you for calling CARE. How may I help you?"

I expected to hear a recording, but instead, sobs came across the line. A weak, desperate voice on the other end said, "I need to schedule my abortion."

I had no clue what to say. I knew if I told her we didn't perform abortions that she would hang up and call the next number. *God, please give me the words to say.*

"Can you tell me why you want to have an abortion?" I asked.

Through waves of sobs, she shared that the father of her baby didn't want it, and she simply could not have this baby all alone. Oh, how my heart broke for her. I could still hear Joe's words, still see his expression when he said he didn't want to be a father.

"I can't schedule an abortion, but if you're willing, I'd love to share my story with you," I said.

She welcomed my story, and we were both in tears as I was able to encourage her and offer resources to support and empower her. In the end, she chose life for her baby. It was unbelievable! Not only would her child live, but she would also be protected from the heartache of abortion.

The calls kept coming. The more I shared my story, the more these calls came straight to my cell phone as personal referrals. In many cases, they came from women who had already suffered the trauma of abortion. I saw women from all backgrounds come through CARE, including pastor's wives, pastor's daughters, and ministry leaders. All were fearful to make that first call or contact. But for those who did, we were able to help them mourn the loss of their children in a safe place. We helped them work through the anger associated with their abortions—the guilt, the unforgiveness, the shame. For a post-abortive woman, there is no bigger shame than that they took the life of their own child. They may have hidden this shame for years—often decades—without ever telling anyone. We helped them acknowledge their sin and heal from it. We helped set them free.

Even those who hadn't wanted their children were still wanted by a God who loved them. A God to whom I would be forever grateful for wanting me and for giving me this ministry.

Chapter 21

Birthdays

The banquet room looked festive with balloons, streamers, and round tables adorned with bright tablecloths. Along the sidewall, a buffet table sagged with hors d'oeuvres and birthday cake.

"Happy birthday," I said, kissing my ninety-year-old grandmother on the cheek before moving on and scanning the room. I saw a relative who looked familiar. Was that him? It had been so long.

"Uncle Dan?" I asked as I approached and caught his eye. I didn't remember him personally, but I knew who he was. Mandy and I had stayed with Uncle Dan as children during one of my mother's stints in jail.

As soon as he saw me, tears began to fill his eyes.

"Billy Jo? I haven't seen you since the day they loaded you up in the car and drove away with you."

"I know. This is crazy after all these years."

He looked me straight in the eye. "We were so heartbroken when they took you and Mandy away. We loved you so much and wanted you to stay with us."

I was shocked. I'd never known this. *Wait a minute. You mean I was wanted?*

"You wanted me? How old was I?"

"Well, let me think. It was 1978, so . . ."

So I had been three years old. That was about right.

Others came bustling in, and the moment was disrupted, but my heart raced, searching for understanding. Was it possible? All these years, that little girl who lived inside me had felt I wasn't wanted. But I was. Someone had wanted me! How did I even process this new information?

I grabbed a slice of birthday cake and saw my cousin Judy across the room. She was a second or third cousin, about my mother's age. We had stayed with her also. With shaking knees and quaking heart, I made my way over to her table. I needed some answers.

"Can I join you?"

"Billy Jo! Of course." She gestured to the chair next to her, and I slid into the seat.

"I wanted to thank you for giving me some of the only joyous and safe times in my childhood." I recounted a memory I had of her teaching me to can tomatoes.

"Those few memories of my time living with you and your husband and Aunt Betty are some of the happiest memories I have of my childhood. Thank you for loving me. You had such an impact on my life."

She reached out and squeezed my hand. "We wanted you. We would have adopted you and kept you forever if we could have."

Again, confirmation. Was I never actually unwanted? Unbeknownst to me, at least two different amazing families had wanted me. I wasn't sure what obstacles had prevented them from adopting Mandy and me, but none of that mattered to my adult heart. *We wanted you.* Those three words were the beginning of me being able to fully and finally thank God for the story I had been given.

This revelation percolated in my heart over the next several months, until my own birthday rolled around. Jay took me out to dinner with the kids and grandkids, as was our tradition. I'm not big on celebrating my birthday. Perhaps it's a feeling that lingers from my childhood, where my existence wasn't celebrated ever, not even on my birthday. Or maybe it's my personality. As an adult, I don't enjoy being the center of attention. I don't want parties celebrating me; I prefer to celebrate privately with my family.

But this day, my grandchildren, Aiden and Annabelle, spilled out of the car in the restaurant parking lot and raced toward me with squeals of "Nana!" If ever someone made me feel adored, it was these two.

I ruffled Aiden's hair as Annabelle hugged my leg. *What a wonderful life I have now.* If anything, my birthday should remind me of how much I have to be grateful for. Jay celebrates me every single day by the way he loves and supports me. I have great relationships with my children and grandchildren, who love to be with me. I serve in a fast-growing, vibrant ministry where I get to be hands on in helping others overcome ugly life experiences with the love of Jesus. I have a core group of amazing friends who share life with me. Sure, I don't have it all together. I struggle like everyone else. I fail sometimes. But this was like living a dream.

We walked inside and sat down at a table, and my mind went back to that other restaurant, to Aiden's birthday, earlier that year. I remembered telling Aiden's birth story and then discovering the fraud of my own.

I had faced a great emotional battle—but the Lord had met me in it, and I heard His still, small voice whispering a gentle reminder to my soul. *My child, just as the details about your grandson's homecoming—the storm, the damage left behind, and the impromptu dinner at Red Lobster—did not define his value, in the same way the circumstances of your birth did not define your value. I did.*

I took a deep breath, remembering Aiden's first breath and the way our hearts had exploded with intense love for his tiny life. Had God felt that way when I was born? It was a love I had never fully been able to embrace for myself. Could I really believe that God loved me and that His love was enough?

I may not have felt it then, but I'd chosen to believe Him, to give Him my deep-seated insecurity and to finally release my birth story to the Lord. So what if there were no earth-shattering events on August 25, 1975, in Westfield, New York? So what if it was just an average, eighty-degree day? That was okay. I didn't need a sports statistic.

As I looked at my family around the table, celebrating my birthday, I realized I now had a *rebirth* story. The plans the Lord had for me from the moment of my first breath—from before my first breath, really— were what had made it a momentous day. His love had given my life significance long before I knew it. Someone had wanted me all along.

Epilogue

Jay is still my best friend, my lover, and my biggest encourager. He has a huge heart for missions and actively serves beside me in whatever the Lord calls us to do. He is a great leader and an amazing husband and father. In 2019 we celebrated our twenty-first wedding anniversary, and he celebrated eighteen years sober. After a career as a stonemason, Jay pursued his passion for guns and now works part time for a gunsmith and full time for a sporting goods store.

Ashlei, after years of rebellion, is now an amazing single mother to my grandchildren, Aiden and Annabelle. She is also a foster mother, currently raising Baby Z until her biological family can care for her or until the Lord makes her ours forever. While Ashlei dropped out of high school to become a mother, she eventually got her GED and her bachelor's degree. She now works full time in adult education as the director of volunteers for the Literacy Council of Tyler, Texas—her dream job. She has recognized that education is key in changing the outcome of many people's lives. Ashlei is a prayer warrior and completely on fire for the Lord.

Austin has been running from all that he knows is good, over the last few years. Thankfully, I have seen glimpses of hope with him recently. While it breaks my heart to watch him suffer, I trust that the Lord is building his testimony even now. Even after all the Lord has done for me and through me, I have a hard time trusting Him with my children, but I know the Lord is not yet finished with my son.

Alex is now twenty years old. During my pregnancy, I prayed that Alex would get the best of Jay and me. We laugh about this now because she is a perfect mixture of us physically and in personality. She is quick witted like Jay and sassy and headstrong like me. She has his top lip, my bottom lip. Even her hair is the perfect combination of mine and his. She has ginormous blue eyes that twinkle with mischief. She is our first child to graduate high school and is now attending college at Jacksonville Baptist College. I am confident the Lord has huge plans for her life.

I am thankful that all three of my children, despite having struggles, do in fact love Jesus and have professed Him as their Lord and Savior.

Mandy continues to be my cheerleader and is proud of me even when my life's calling goes beyond her own comfort zone. She loves me like crazy, and though me telling my story is painful for her, she has loved me each step of this journey, filling in timelines and details my mind could not remember. Mandy has never stopped wanting to protect me, and I thank God for giving her to me as my big sister.

Jackie lost her husband Ed to cancer and eventually came to know the Lord. Because Jackie is living in a nursing home with declining health and limited mobility, her walk with the Lord is not what it once was, but I do know her relationship with Him is genuine.

I am truly proud to be part of the Garrett family. Though they initially didn't want Jay and me to be together, GaGa later shared sweet praises for me and the blessing I have brought to the Garrett family. To know that this highly respectable lover of Jesus was proud to be my grandmother meant the whole stinking world to me. GaGa passed away a few years ago and is living life abundantly with our Lord and

Epilogue

Savior, reunited with her beloved son (Jay's dad) and her husband (Jay's granddad).

Marilyn and I are still friends, but as seasons come and go, she is not a part of my central circle of daily activity anymore. We attend different churches and we serve in different ministries, but her lessons stay ever present in my heart and mind. I have never had to wonder what I did wrong or question why God "took her away," because she prepared me for friends and circumstances to come and go from my life. We do still send prayer requests to each other regularly; we just have a different relationship today than we did back then. She has mentored innumerable women over the years, and I hope to make her proud by living my life in a way that honors the Jesus she so gracefully and boldly taught me about.

Acknowledgments

To my husband, Jay. I cannot adequately express my appreciation to you for always supporting me telling my story. You've held me while I cried, kissed away my fears, and never stopped encouraging me.

To my girls, Ashlei and Alexandria, who would not let me give in or give up no matter how much I doubted and struggled—thank you.

To Austin, for believing in me even if knowing my secrets is not on your most-wanted list.

To my sister-in-law, Penny—your support through this whole process has been most unexpected and touching. Your excitement and backing from the moment you found out about this book have been a major driving force to the finish line. I am so glad I married your brother and that you are now my sister!

To Karen—you believed in me when I did not have the faith to believe in myself. I am not sure I would have taken the leap of faith to write this without you pushing me.

To Naomi, my night-owl wordsmithing friend who always answered my pleas for help. Whether by sending prayers, helping me describe what needed to be written, or simply offering a word of encouragement when I wanted to quit, I could not have made it through this without you.

To my inner circle of friends—you know who you are. You listened to me cry, whine, and throw temper tantrums, and still you gave, prayed, and supported me during this long process. Again, there are no words to express my gratitude.

To Sarah, my writing coach and editor—the one who knew what to ask and how to help me tell my story. You got inside my heart and helped me express my thoughts so perfectly. I will always cherish you and appreciate what you have done for me in helping make *Unwanted No More* what it is today.

To Athena—thank you for believing in my story and for giving me the avenue to share it with others.

And above all, to Jesus, my Lord, for never stopping the pursuit of my heart. You have captured it completely. My life is Yours.

Do You Know My Jesus?

Maybe, like me, you have always believed in God or a "higher power," or maybe the idea of a loving God is about as foreign to you as anything you can imagine. I do not want you to close this book without the same opportunity that was once given to me. Do you know Jesus as your Lord and Savior? Have you made a personal, heartfelt commitment to follow Him? I cannot pretend to know all the rules, but I know this for certain: if you believe with all your heart that Jesus is real; that He is the Son of God; that He lived a perfect, sinless life and then died in your place to pay for your sins; and that if you ask Him to forgive you and to save you, He is faithful to do just that. Below you will see a simple sample of a prayer like the one I once said as I was begging God to be real in my life. Please know this—the words you say are far less important than the desire of your heart. The words will not be what save you. Your belief in Jesus Christ as your Lord is what will make you new. So in as much faith as you can muster, even if, like me, you are simply begging God to be real, I implore you to say a prayer like this:

Lord Jesus, I need You. I know I'm a sinner, and I thank You for dying on the cross to pay for my sins. I open the door of my heart and receive You as my Savior. I believe Jesus Christ is Your Son. I believe that He died for my sin and that You raised Him to life. From this day forward, I surrender my life to You. I pray this in the name of Jesus. Amen.

Order Information

To order additional copies of this book, please visit
www.redemption-press.com.
Also available on Amazon.com and BarnesandNoble.com
Or by calling toll free 1-844-2REDEEM.